Economics of Banking and Money
Insight into Power, Trust, and Change

By Willem Tait

"This book reveals where money comes from and how to grow it. Join me on a journey of discovery, manipulation, and strategy. You'll thank me later."

— *Willem Tait*

Copyright © 2024 by Willem Tait - All rights reserved.

Copyright Warning

No part of this publication may be reproduced, distributed, or transmitted in any form or by any means, including photocopying, recording, or other electronic or mechanical methods, without the prior written permission of the author, except in the case of brief quotations embodied in reviews and certain other noncommercial uses permitted by copyright law.

For permission requests, contact the author at:
willemtait@outlook.com

Disclaimer

This eBook is for educational and informational purposes only. The author is not liable for any damages or losses arising from the use or misuse of the content.

Cover Design: Time Brands
Published by WRT Publishing
First Edition

LinkedIn: https://www.linkedin.com/in/willemtait/
X (previously Twitter): https://x.com/willemtait
Calendly: https://calendly.com/willemtait

KDP Amazon ISBN Paperback: 9798303738201
KDP Amazon ISBN Hardcover: 9798303741928
Library Print ISBN: 978-1-0370-3805-1
Library Ebook ISBN: 978-1-0370-3806-8

Preface

Money is more than just numbers in a ledger or notes in your wallet, it's the heartbeat of our global economy, a force that shapes nations, drives innovation, and impacts every aspect of our lives. Yet, for many, the world of money and banking feels like an enigma, complex, daunting, and out of reach. That's why I wrote *The Economics of Banking and Money*.

This book is your compass through the fascinating evolution of money, from bartering goods in ancient marketplaces to the revolutionary rise of digital currencies.

Each chapter uncovers the pivotal milestones that have transformed how we trade, save, and invest, offering a narrative that blends historical insights with a forward-looking perspective on the financial systems that underpin our world.

Whether you're a curious student, a professional navigating the financial sector, or someone simply intrigued by how money moves and evolves, this book is designed to empower you.

It unravels complex ideas, making them accessible and engaging, while providing practical insights into topics ranging from central banking and inflation to the psychology of money and the promise of blockchain technology.

But this isn't just a book about systems and institutions; it's a story about people, about trust, innovation, and resilience. It explores how human ingenuity has shaped economic frameworks and how those frameworks, in turn, shape our societies. From the triumphs of cooperative banking to the lessons learned from financial crises, the journey through these pages will deepen your understanding of how money influences our lives and our futures.

I am deeply grateful to the scholars, practitioners, and visionaries whose insights have informed my thinking, and to my family, friends, and mentors who have supported me every step of the way.

Writing this book has been a journey of discovery, and I hope it sparks the same sense of curiosity and inspiration in you as it did in me.

As we stand on the cusp of rapid financial and technological transformation, understanding the past and present of money and banking has never been more critical.

My hope is that this book not only informs but also motivates you to engage actively with the systems that shape our world.

Together, let's explore the dynamic interplay of economics, trust, and innovation that defines the story of money.

Welcome to this exploration. Let's begin.

Introduction

Imagine standing in a bustling marketplace thousands of years ago, watching people trade livestock for grain or tools for cloth. Fast forward to today, where a tap of your smartphone can send money across continents in seconds. How did we get here? What forces turned basic barter systems into a global network of banking and commerce? And more importantly, where are we headed next?

These are the questions that drive this book. The story of money and banking is not just a historical account or a study of economics; it's a lens through which we can understand human progress. From the shimmering gold coins of ancient empires to the intangible codes of Bitcoin, every transformation in the way we use money reflects a deeper evolution in society, in trust, technology, and ambition.

But this journey is not without its challenges. Financial crises, corruption, and inequality have cast long shadows over the world of money. Understanding these pitfalls is as crucial as celebrating the innovations, for it is through this balance that we learn to navigate an increasingly complex financial landscape.

In this book, you will uncover the mechanisms that make our economic systems tick, the pulse of central banks, the flow of money supply, and the psychological forces that drive our financial decisions. You will also explore the cutting-edge technologies that promise to reshape the future of finance, from blockchain to decentralized finance (DeFi). More than just learning the mechanics, you will see how these systems affect people's lives, your life, every single day.

This is not just a book for economists or bankers. It's for anyone who has ever wondered why prices rise, how banks work, or what the future of money might look like. It's for the student seeking clarity, the professional craving insight, and the curious mind eager to connect the dots in our ever-changing financial world.

Let this introduction be your invitation to think critically, to question assumptions, and to embrace the complexities of money and banking with curiosity and confidence. As you turn the pages, remember: the story of money is, at its heart, a story about us, our choices, our innovations, and our collective future. Let's dive in.

Table of Contents

Preface 2
Introduction 5
Table of Contents 7
CHAPTER 1: The Evolution of Money: From Barter to Bitcoin 11
    Bartering 11
    Gold Coins 12
    Paper Money 13
    Fiat Currency 13
    Digital Money 14
    Conclusion: Key Takeaways and Insights 17
CHAPTER 2: The Role of Banks Beyond the Vault . 20
    Deposits 20
    Fractional Reserve Banking 21
    Regulations 22
    Technology 24
    Conclusion: Key Takeaways and Insights 25
CHAPTER 3: Supply, Demand, and the Flow of Money 28
    Circulation of Money 28
    Supply and Demand 29
    Inflation and Deflation 30
    Market Forces 31
    Global Scale 32
    Conclusion: Key Takeaways and Insights 34
CHAPTER 4: Central Banks - The Economy's Invisible Hand 37

Interest Rates and Monetary Policy 37
Inflation Control 38
Money Supply 38
Trust Management 39
Global Trade 40
Conclusion: Key Takeaways and Insights 42
CHAPTER 5: Booms, Busts, and Banking Crises ... 45
Rhythm and Cycles 45
Systemic Risk 46
Ripple Effect 48
Conclusion: Key Takeaways and Insights 50
CHAPTER 6: Global Money: Trade, Exchange, and Power 53
How Money Moves 53
Currency Valuation 54
Globalization 55
Conclusion: Key Takeaways and Insights 58
CHAPTER 7: The Technology Revolution: Digital Currencies and Beyond 61
Accessibility and Convenience 61
Blockchain 62
Cryptocurrencies 63
Decentralized Finance 64
Fintech 64
Conclusion: Key Takeaways and Insights 66
CHAPTER 8: The Future of Money and Banking: Trust, Innovation, and Change 71
Faster and Cheaper 71
Sustainability 72

Trust 73
Adaptability 73
Societal Values 74
Globalization 74
Conclusion: Key Takeaways and Insights 77
CHAPTER 9: The Psychology of Money: Why We Spend, Save, and Invest 80
Behavioral Economics 80
Cognitive Biases 81
Financial Literacy 83
Conclusion: Key Takeaways and Insights 85
CHAPTER 10: The Dark Side of Money and Banking: Scandals, Corruption, and Crime 90
Libor Scandal 90
HSBC 91
Nick Leeson and Barings Bank 91
Systemic Risk 92
Conclusion: Key Takeaways and Insights 94
CHAPTER 11: How to Weather Economic Storms .. 98
Emergency Fund 100
Diversification 101
Smart Management 103
Understanding Regulations and Policies 106
Adaptability 107
Sustainability 108
Financial Resilience 108
Conclusion: Key Takeaways and Insights 110
CHAPTER 12: Success Stories 116
Iceland 116

    The United Arab Emirates 119
    Mobile Banking In Africa 122
    Post Covid-19 Policies.. 125
    Cooperative Banking 129
    Green Initiatives... 134
    Conclusion: Key Takeaways and Insights 138
CHAPTER 13: Shadow Banking 142
    Credit, Liquidity, and Funding 142
    Higher Risk Loans and Niche Markets 143
    Market Makers 144
    Risk and Reward 144
    Fairness and Access 145
    Conclusion: Key Takeaways and Insights 147
CHAPTER 14: Conclusion and Reflection............... 152
    Pause and Reflect 152
    Summary of Chapters... 152
    Your Journey Continues 157
Updated List of Books to Date 161
    Real Estate Mastery Books Series 164
Acknowledgement.. 165
Social Profiles.. 166
Mentorship, Coaching, Consulting and Public Speaking.. 167
About the Author 169
    We Value Your Feedback!.................................... 171
    Portfolio of Books by Willem Tait.......................... 172

CHAPTER 1: The Evolution of Money: From Barter to Bitcoin

If you think about it, money is one of humanity's greatest inventions. It's so deeply ingrained in our lives that imagining a world without it feels almost impossible.

Bartering

But there was a time when money, as we know it, didn't exist. Back then, people got by with bartering, trading one good for another. You might offer a basket of apples to your neighbor in exchange for a sack of grain. Simple enough, right?

But what happened when your neighbor didn't need apples or, worse, didn't like them? The whole system fell apart.

That's the first problem money solved: it gave us a universal medium of exchange, something everyone could agree had value. Bartering worked, but it was clunky.

Imagine trying to trade a cow for a dozen pots, you'd need someone who not only had pots but also wanted your cow. This double coincidence of wants was rare, making trade inefficient. That's when commodity money came into the picture. Commodity money was any object that had intrinsic value and was widely accepted in trade. Think of items like gold, silver, or even salt. These goods weren't just useful for exchange; they had value beyond the transaction. Gold, for instance, was prized for its beauty and rarity, while salt was essential for preserving food. Commodity money smoothed out the rough edges of barter by giving people something tangible and widely desirable to trade.

Gold Coins

As societies grew more complex, carrying around heavy bags of gold or bulky sacks of salt became impractical. Enter the invention of coins, standardized pieces of metal stamped with a government's seal. These coins represented a specific value, making transactions quicker and more trustworthy. A gold coin could buy you bread in one town and silk in another, and you didn't have to argue about its worth. The idea of trust began to play a crucial role here. People trusted the coin's stamp, believing it guaranteed the coin's value. Without this trust, even the most beautiful gold coin would be just another shiny object.

Paper Money

This trust carried over into the next big leap: paper money. The story of paper currency begins in China, where merchants started using promissory notes to avoid carrying heavy coins. Eventually, governments adopted the practice, printing paper that could be exchanged for a certain amount of gold or silver. This was the birth of the gold standard, where every paper note was backed by a physical reserve of precious metal. It worked because people believed in the system. They trusted that a dollar in their hand could be exchanged for gold in a vault somewhere. This trust was essential because, in reality, the paper itself was worthless.

Fiat Currency

But even the gold standard had its limits. During times of war or economic stress, governments often printed more money than they had gold to back it. This led to inflation, eroding trust in the system. Eventually, most countries abandoned the gold standard, shifting to what we call fiat currency. Unlike commodity money, fiat currency has no intrinsic value. Its worth comes entirely from government decree and public trust. A $20 bill is valuable not because of the paper it's printed on but because we all agree it is. This shared belief makes modern economies possible.

Fiat currency changed the game in many ways. It gave governments more control over their economies, allowing them to manage inflation and respond to financial crises. But it also raised new questions. What happens when people lose trust in their currency? We've seen this play out in countries like Zimbabwe and Venezuela, where hyperinflation rendered money almost worthless. In such cases, people often revert to bartering or using alternative forms of money, like foreign currencies or even goods.

Digital Money

The digital age brought yet another revolution in the evolution of money. With the rise of online banking and electronic payments, money became less about physical cash and more about numbers on a screen. Today, most of the money in circulation isn't tangible; it exists as digital entries in bank accounts. You can transfer thousands of dollars with a few taps on your phone, and it all happens invisibly. This convenience has reshaped how we think about and interact with money.

And then came cryptocurrencies, the latest chapter in this long journey.

Bitcoin, the first cryptocurrency, was introduced in 2009 as a decentralized form of money. Unlike fiat currency, Bitcoin isn't controlled by any government or central authority. Instead, it operates on blockchain technology, a decentralized ledger that records all transactions transparently and securely. Bitcoin and its successors promised to solve some of fiat currency's problems, like inflation and lack of privacy. But they also raised new challenges, such as volatility and regulatory concerns.

Cryptocurrencies are fascinating because they challenge our traditional ideas about money. If money is based on trust, as we've seen throughout history, then Bitcoin asks us to trust technology instead of institutions. For some, this is a liberating idea. For others, it's unsettling. Either way, cryptocurrencies have forced us to reconsider what money can and should be in a digital world.

Throughout this evolution, one thing has remained constant: the need for trust. Whether it's trusting a neighbor to trade fairly, a government to back its currency, or a blockchain to secure transactions, trust is the invisible thread that holds the system together. Without it, money loses its meaning. This brings us back to the core idea that money isn't just a tool for exchange; it's a social agreement, a collective belief that drives economies and shapes societies.

Conclusion: Key Takeaways and Insights

As we move forward, the story of money continues to unfold, weaving together threads of history, technology, and human innovation.

Money has never been static; it evolves with our societies, adapting to new needs and challenges while reflecting the changes in how we live, trade, and connect. From ancient systems of bartering goods to the complexities of global financial markets, every chapter in this story has contributed to shaping the world as we know it today. New technologies, economic shifts, and global challenges will undoubtedly shape its next chapters, presenting both opportunities and risks. But understanding its past, from bartering sheep to trading Bitcoin, gives us a powerful lens to better view the present and anticipate the future.

Each step in money's evolution reflects not only our ingenuity but also our resilience and adaptability. The transition from gold coins to paper currency, and now to digital wallets and cryptocurrencies, shows how we continually redefine value and trust to meet the demands of an ever-changing world. These changes are not just about practicality; they reveal deeper truths about human behavior, innovation, and the systems we create to foster stability and growth.

Money is more than a medium of exchange, it is a living reflection of our ability to solve problems and build connections.

Yet, money does not operate in isolation. Its journey is closely tied to the institutions we've built to manage and regulate it, none more significant than banks. The next step in our journey will delve into the pivotal role of banks, the institutions that have become both the guardians and creators of money. What began as humble repositories for valuables has evolved into a cornerstone of modern economies. Banks do far more than simply hold money; they lend it, invest it, and in many ways, create it through mechanisms like fractional reserve banking.

Banks influence the flow of money, determining where it goes and who has access to it. Their decisions ripple through economies, shaping everything from small businesses to global trade. They stand at the intersection of trust and power, managing risk while driving growth. These institutions are central to the story of money, serving as both enablers of opportunity and sources of economic influence.

Understanding the evolution of institutions, their functions, and their impact is essential to grasping the full picture of how economies thrive or falter

As we turn to the next chapter, we'll uncover the fascinating journey of banking, how did a simple idea of safekeeping evolve into the sophisticated financial ecosystems we depend on today? Have you ever stopped to think about how banks shape nearly every aspect of our daily lives, from the money in our wallets to the stability of entire economies?

By exploring their role, we unlock a deeper understanding of the systems that keep the world turning and the trust that binds it all together. Get ready to dive into the captivating story of banks and discover their profound impact on the world of money. You might never look at your bank the same way again!

CHAPTER 2: The Role of Banks Beyond the Vault

When you think of a bank, the first image that likely comes to mind is a sturdy building with a vault. Maybe you picture rows of tellers, ATMs, or even the app on your phone where you check your balance. But banks are so much more than these outward features. In reality, they are the engine rooms of modern economies, quietly working behind the scenes to connect people who have money with people who need it.

This simple-sounding role, called financial intermediation, is the foundation of their power and influence.

Deposits

Let's start with deposits. When you deposit money into a savings or checking account, it doesn't just sit there gathering dust. Instead, your bank takes a portion of that money and lends it to someone else. This could be a small business owner looking to expand, a family buying their first home, or even a student taking out a loan for college. In doing so, the bank transforms your idle savings into active capital that fuels economic growth. It's a delicate balance, though, because the bank also needs to make sure it has enough funds on hand to meet the needs of depositors who want to withdraw their money.

Fractional Reserve Banking

This is where fractional reserve banking comes into play. Banks are not required to keep all your deposits in their vaults. Instead, they hold a fraction, often just a small percentage, and lend out the rest. This system allows banks to multiply the money supply, creating credit that powers everything from individual purchases to large-scale investments. Imagine you deposit $1,000 in your bank. The bank might keep $100 in reserve and lend out the remaining $900 to someone else. That $900 might then be deposited into another bank, which repeats the process, creating even more credit. This is how banks effectively "create" money, a concept tied to the trust we explored in the previous chapter.

But creating money isn't the only thing banks do. They also play a crucial role in determining who gets access to credit and on what terms.

This decision-making power gives banks incredible influence over economic development. A bank's willingness to lend to a new entrepreneur could lead to the next breakthrough innovation. Conversely, withholding credit from struggling businesses during tough times can exacerbate economic downturns. Banks walk a tightrope, balancing their role as profit-driven businesses with their responsibility to contribute to economic stability.

Regulations

Regulation is a key factor in ensuring banks don't overstep or jeopardize the financial system.

Governments and central banks impose rules to keep banks in check, requiring them to hold minimum reserves and undergo regular audits. These regulations are designed to prevent reckless lending and protect depositors. The 2008 financial crisis serves as a stark reminder of what can happen when banks operate without sufficient oversight. Back then, excessive risk-taking and poor regulation led to widespread bank failures, wiping out savings and destabilizing economies worldwide. Trust in banking took a serious hit, and rebuilding it required massive intervention and stricter regulations.

Trust remains the cornerstone of banking. When you deposit money, you trust that it will be available when you need it.

When you take out a loan, the bank trusts you'll repay it with interest. This mutual trust is what keeps the system running smoothly. Without it, the entire structure collapses, as seen in historical bank runs where fear and panic caused people to withdraw their money en masse. Modern safeguards, like deposit insurance, exist to prevent such scenarios and reassure people that their money is safe.

Banks don't just serve individuals; they're deeply entwined with businesses and governments as well.

For businesses, banks provide essential services like payroll management, business loans, and cash flow solutions. For governments, banks help manage national debt, distribute public funds, and stabilize the economy during crises. During the COVID-19 pandemic, for example, many governments partnered with banks to distribute emergency funds to citizens and small businesses. These partnerships highlight the indispensable role banks play in both normal and extraordinary times.

Technology

Technology has also reshaped banking in profound ways. Online banking, mobile apps, and digital wallets have made managing money more convenient than ever. But these innovations also bring challenges, such as cybersecurity risks and competition from fintech startups. Despite these disruptions, traditional banks remain vital, largely because of the trust they've built over centuries. However, as we'll see in a later chapter on technology, the future of banking may look very different as these trends continue to evolve.

Conclusion: Key Takeaways and Insights

Understanding the role of banks helps us see why they're often referred to as the "lifeblood" of the economy. They don't just store money; they move it, grow it, and decide where it flows.

A deposit made in one town could fund a new business halfway across the country, while a loan granted to a farmer might enable the production of food that nourishes a city.

Their impact is everywhere, from the mortgages that build our homes to the investments that drive technological breakthroughs and fund the next wave of innovation. This interconnectedness underscores not only their importance but also their vulnerability.

When banks succeed, economies thrive.

They foster job creation, support businesses, and enable communities to grow. But when they falter, the consequences ripple far and wide, affecting everyone from small businesses to global markets. A single misstep, whether it's poor risk management or a loss of trust, can disrupt the delicate balance that keeps the financial system functioning. The 2008 financial crisis serves as a stark reminder of this, showing how deeply banking failures can impact ordinary lives, from lost homes to shuttered businesses.

Banks are more than just institutions; they are central nodes in the complex web of money's movement.

They facilitate trade, connect savers with borrowers, and help governments manage economic policies. This role gives them immense power but also places significant responsibility on their shoulders. When banks manage their functions effectively, they act as catalysts for growth and stability. But when mismanaged, they can become sources of systemic risk, jeopardizing entire economies.

As we move to the next chapter, it's time to shift our focus from the institutions themselves to the broader picture of money's movement.

How does money circulate within an economy, and what forces determine its flow? What happens when demand outstrips supply, or when money becomes stagnant? These questions are at the heart of understanding economic systems, revealing the intricate dance between supply, demand, and the decisions we all make with our money.

This exploration will uncover the forces that drive spending, saving, and investment, and how these individual actions shape broader economic trends. Understanding these dynamics will help us grasp the delicate balance that keeps economies in motion, from bustling marketplaces to global trade networks.

Let's now take a closer look at how money moves from one pocket to another, what fuels its journey, and how does this movement shape the growth and stability of economies both big and small? Have you ever wondered what invisible forces guide this flow and why some economies thrive while others falter? Understanding the pathways of money unlocks a deeper appreciation for the systems that underpin our daily lives. In the next chapter, we'll delve into the mechanisms and networks that facilitate this flow, uncovering the intricate web of connections that drive global financial interactions. Prepare to be amazed by the complexity and ingenuity behind the movement of money!

CHAPTER 3: Supply, Demand, and the Flow of Money

Money is like water, constantly moving and shaping the economy with every ripple. It doesn't sit still; it flows from one hand to another, through businesses, households, and governments, influencing decisions at every turn.

Circulation of Money

This circulation is what keeps an economy alive. Just like blood carries nutrients in the body, money carries value, ensuring goods and services reach those who need them. But what drives this flow? The answer lies in the forces of supply and demand, the spending and saving decisions of individuals, and the ever-present tug-of-war between inflation and deflation.

Every dollar you spend contributes to economic activity. When you buy a loaf of bread, you're not just feeding yourself; you're supporting the baker, the farmer who grew the wheat, and the delivery driver who brought the bread to the store.

Multiply transactions by millions of transactions, and you have an economy in motion.

But what if everyone decided to save their money instead of spending it? While saving is essential for individual security, too much of it at once can slow the economy. When people save instead of spend, businesses see lower demand for their products, leading to reduced production, fewer jobs, and ultimately, a sluggish economy.

This delicate balance between spending and saving is at the heart of economic health. Saving is beneficial for individuals but can hurt the economy if practiced collectively. During economic booms, people tend to spend more, fueling growth. Conversely, in times of uncertainty, like recessions, people save more, causing demand to drop. Governments and central banks step in during such times to encourage spending, often by lowering interest rates or injecting money into the economy, a topic we'll revisit when discussing central banks.

Supply and Demand

Supply and demand are the twin engines that power the flow of money. Think about it: when demand for a product rises, businesses have an incentive to produce more. This often leads to higher prices, as consumers are willing to pay a premium for scarce goods. On the flip side, when demand falls, prices drop, sometimes below the cost of production, forcing businesses to cut back or close shop.

Fluctuations are a natural part of any economy, but they can cause disruptions if not managed carefully.

Inflation and Deflation

Inflation and deflation play significant roles in this story. Inflation, the general rise in prices over time, erodes the purchasing power of money. It's why a dollar today doesn't buy as much as it did a decade ago. Moderate inflation is often seen as a sign of a healthy economy, signaling growth and increased demand.

However, too much inflation, like what happens during hyperinflation, can destabilize economies.

Deflation, or falling prices, might sound like a good thing, but it can be just as harmful. When prices drop, people tend to delay purchases, expecting even lower prices in the future. This lack of spending slows economic activity and can lead to a downward spiral.

Money supply, controlled by central banks, directly impacts these forces. Too much money in circulation can lead to inflation, while too little can stifle growth and trigger deflation. It's a balancing act, requiring careful adjustments to ensure the economy stays on track. Fractional reserve banking creates money. That process feeds into the money supply, amplifying its effects on the economy. The choices banks make about lending, combined with the spending habits of consumers, create a complex web of interactions that drive the economy forward.

Market Forces

Market forces also come into play. In free-market economies, supply and demand are largely driven by individual decisions. What you choose to buy, where you shop, and even what you invest in send signals to businesses about what's valuable. These signals influence how resources are allocated, which industries grow, and which ones fade away.

In more controlled economies, governments play a larger role in directing the flow of money, but even they must consider the fundamentals of supply and demand.

All of this ties back to trust, the invisible force we've discussed in previous chapters. Without trust in the value of money, the entire system falters. If people believe prices will keep rising uncontrollably or that their savings will lose value, confidence erodes, and the economy can spiral into chaos.

Similarly, if banks and businesses can't trust that consumers will spend or repay loans, they pull back, further slowing the flow of money.

It's a delicate ecosystem, one that depends on confidence at every level.

Global Scale

This intricate dance of supply, demand, and money circulation isn't confined to individual economies. On a global scale, trade and currency exchange bring another layer of complexity. Money flows across borders, influenced by trade agreements, currency values, and geopolitical events. A strong demand for one country's exports can boost its economy, while a lack of demand can lead to stagnation. These global connections, which we'll explore in more detail later, underscore the interconnected nature of modern economies.

Understanding the flow of money gives us a clearer picture of how economies function and why balance is so critical.

Conclusion: Key Takeaways and Insights

Spend too freely, and you risk inflation. Prices rise, purchasing power diminishes, and the cost of living spirals upward, straining households and destabilizing economies. Save too much, and you risk stagnation. When money is hoarded instead of spent or invested, demand dries up, businesses scale back, and economic growth slows.

These principles don't just apply to individuals; governments and businesses face the same delicate balancing act. A government that overspends risks burdening future generations with debt, while one that underspends may fail to stimulate its economy during downturns. Similarly, businesses must allocate their resources wisely, ensuring they have enough cash flow to weather challenges while investing strategically for growth.

It's a dynamic system, constantly adapting to new challenges and opportunities.

Technological advancements, global trade, and geopolitical shifts all influence how money moves and how economies respond. One misstep, whether it's excessive spending, poor investment choices, or a lack of strategic planning, can have far-reaching consequences. This interplay between spending and saving, risk and reward, highlights the need for institutions capable of steering the economy through unpredictable waters.

As we turn our focus to the next chapter, we'll explore the vital role of central banks in managing these delicate balances.

Acting as the referees of this economic game, they wield powerful tools like interest rates and monetary policy to keep the flow of money steady. By raising or lowering interest rates, central banks can influence borrowing and spending behaviors, nudging economies toward growth or cooling them down to prevent overheating. They also oversee the money supply, ensuring that there's enough liquidity in the system to keep commerce flowing without triggering runaway inflation.

Central banks hold immense influence over our daily lives in ways we often don't even realize.

From the price of groceries to the cost of borrowing for a new home, their decisions ripple through every corner of the economy. These institutions stand at the intersection of trust and power, tasked with balancing the needs of individuals, businesses, and governments. Understanding their role gives us deeper insight into the forces that shape our financial lives and helps us appreciate the complexity of the systems that keep economies functioning.

Let's dive into the fascinating world of central banks and discover how these powerful institutions shape the global economy. Ever wondered who keeps the financial system stable during a crisis or how money supply and interest rates are controlled? Central banks are the hidden architects of economic stability, responding to challenges with strategies that impact every one of us.

Their role is not just pivotal, it's extraordinary. In the next chapter, we'll explore the innovative tools and strategies they use to influence monetary policy and guide economies through uncertain times. Get ready to uncover the secrets behind the decisions that drive prosperity and build trust in financial systems worldwide.

CHAPTER 4: Central Banks - The Economy's Invisible Hand

If you imagine the economy as a grand orchestra, the central bank is its conductor, quietly ensuring harmony among the many instruments. Its role is rarely flashy, but the impact is undeniable.

Interest Rates and Monetary Policy

Central banks like the Federal Reserve in the United States hold the reins of the economy, using tools like interest rates and monetary policy to strike a delicate balance between growth and stability. While they don't dictate every note, their influence guides the tempo of economic activity, ensuring the music doesn't spiral into chaos or grind to a halt.

One of the central bank's most powerful tools is the control of interest rates.

These are the rates at which banks borrow money from one another or the central bank itself. When interest rates are low, borrowing becomes cheaper, encouraging businesses and individuals to take out loans and spend more. This stimulates economic growth, creating jobs and boosting demand. On the other hand, high interest rates discourage borrowing and spending, slowing down an overheated economy. It's a balancing act aimed at preventing extreme inflation or deflation, both of which can wreak havoc on financial systems.

Inflation Control

Inflation control is a core responsibility of central banks. A little inflation is like seasoning, it adds flavor to economic growth. But too much of it, and the economy becomes overheated, with prices rising faster than incomes. Left unchecked, inflation erodes the value of money, making everyday goods and services unaffordable for many. Conversely, deflation, the opposite of inflation, can stall economic activity, as people delay purchases in anticipation of falling prices. Central banks aim for a sweet spot, often around 2% inflation annually, a level that encourages spending without reducing the purchasing power of money too quickly.

Money Supply

The money supply is another critical lever for central banks. By increasing or decreasing the amount of money circulating in the economy, they can influence spending, saving, and investment behaviors. For instance, during the 2008 financial crisis, the Federal Reserve introduced quantitative easing, injecting money into the economy to encourage lending and investment. While effective in jumpstarting economic activity, such measures are not without risks, as they can lead to excessive inflation or asset bubbles if overused.

Trust Management

Trust, as we've seen in earlier chapters, is central to the success of any financial system. Central banks play a pivotal role in maintaining this trust. They are designed to be independent of political pressures, allowing them to focus on long-term stability rather than short-term gains. This independence helps reinforce public confidence that decisions are made in the economy's best interest, not swayed by political agendas.

However, this trust is fragile, requiring transparency and effective communication to sustain.

Take the Federal Reserve as an example. Often referred to simply as "the Fed," it operates with a dual mandate: to promote maximum employment and stable prices. This dual responsibility requires a careful juggling act. When unemployment rises, the Fed might lower interest rates to encourage businesses to hire more workers. But if prices start rising too quickly, it must pivot, raising rates to cool down inflation. These decisions are based on complex data, market trends, and sometimes, gut instincts informed by years of expertise.

Global Trade

Central banks are not just national players; they also influence global economies. In an interconnected world, decisions made by the Federal Reserve or the European Central Bank can send ripples across borders. For instance, when the Fed raises interest rates, it often strengthens the U.S. dollar, making American exports more expensive for other countries. This can affect global trade balances and even trigger economic challenges in emerging markets that rely on dollar-denominated debt. Central banks, therefore, must consider the international ramifications of their actions, even while prioritizing domestic stability.

Critics of central banks often argue that their immense power lacks sufficient checks and balances.

After all, their decisions can impact everything from mortgage rates to the price of groceries. Others question whether central banks always act swiftly or effectively enough in times of crisis. These criticisms highlight the challenges central banks face in balancing their roles as guardians of the economy and responsive leaders in a fast-changing financial landscape.

The influence of central banks extends beyond crises. In times of steady growth, their actions might seem mundane, even invisible, as they fine-tune policies to keep the economy on track. But their role becomes unmistakable during turbulent times, whether it's responding to a global pandemic, a financial meltdown, or the threat of runaway inflation. Their ability to act decisively and instill confidence can mean the difference between recovery and prolonged economic hardship.

Conclusion: Key Takeaways and Insights

The role of central banks underscores the deep interconnectedness of financial systems we've been exploring throughout this journey. These institutions stand as pivotal anchors in the economic landscape, shaping the flow of money and ensuring stability amidst constant change.

From managing the money supply to controlling inflation, their actions ripple through economies, influencing everything from household budgets to global trade.

Central banks don't just react to economic conditions, they actively shape them, fostering growth in some areas while reining in excesses in others. This delicate balance ties directly to the trust we place in economic systems, which rely on these institutions to act as stewards of stability and progress.

By adjusting interest rates, monitoring inflation, and managing liquidity, central banks influence the decisions of individuals, businesses, and governments alike. Whether it's encouraging borrowing to fuel growth or tightening policies to cool down an overheating economy, their actions are interconnected with every level of financial activity.

This web of influence extends beyond national borders, affecting global trade, investment flows, and currency exchanges. In an increasingly globalized world, the actions of one central bank can have profound consequences for others, highlighting just how tightly intertwined modern economies have become.

As we continue, we'll dive deeper into how this interconnectedness plays out on a global scale.

Money doesn't stop at borders; it moves seamlessly across nations, driven by the forces of trade, investment, and geopolitical relationships. How does the value of one currency affect another? What happens when a country experiences a trade surplus or deficit? These questions reveal the complex interplay of international trade and foreign exchange markets.

Understanding these dynamics is key to appreciating the full scope of money's movement.

The flow of global money connects economies in ways that are both exciting and precarious. Trade agreements, currency valuations, and financial policies form a delicate web where the actions of one country can create ripples, or waves, in others.

As we step into the next chapter, have you ever wondered how money flows seamlessly across borders, connecting economies and shaping the global marketplace? We'll unravel the fascinating complexities of international trade and exchange, uncovering the hidden forces that drive these vital connections. What makes one currency rise while another falls, and how do these movements impact businesses and individuals worldwide?

By understanding these intricate global ties, we gain the tools to navigate a world where money truly knows no borders, and to seize the opportunities that come with it. Get ready to explore the dynamic dance of global finance and discover the power it holds to transform economies and lives!

CHAPTER 5: Booms, Busts, and Banking Crises

Economic cycles are as old as economies themselves, swinging like a pendulum between prosperity and hardship. There's a natural rhythm to these cycles: Periods of growth and optimism, followed by downturns and corrections.

Rhythm and Cycles

It's during these downturns that banking crises often rear their ugly heads, leaving behind a trail of financial ruin and shaken confidence. History has shown us that while booms can feel exhilarating, the busts that follow often remind us just how fragile the system can be. Yet, every crisis offers lessons, shaping the way banks, governments, and individuals approach the future.

At the heart of many economic crises are financial bubbles. A bubble forms when the price of an asset, whether it's real estate, stocks, or even tulips (as in the famous Dutch Tulip Mania), rises far beyond its intrinsic value. Fueled by speculation and exuberance, people pour money into the asset, driving prices even higher. Eventually, the bubble bursts, and prices come crashing down. The aftermath can be devastating, especially when banks are deeply entangled in the bubble, having lent money to fuel the frenzy.

The 2008 financial crisis stands as a stark example of this dynamic. Leading up to the crisis, housing prices in the United States skyrocketed, driven by subprime mortgages and risky financial instruments tied to them. Banks and financial institutions, eager to profit, took on enormous risks without fully understanding the consequences. When housing prices fell, the system unraveled. Major banks faced insolvency, credit markets froze, and economies around the world spiraled into recession.

It wasn't just a banking collapse, it was a collapse of trust in the financial system itself.

Systemic Risk

Risk management is supposed to be the safety net that prevents such disasters, but it often falls short in the face of greed and overconfidence. Banks have risk assessment teams and regulations designed to ensure stability, but no system is foolproof. The interconnectedness of global banking means that a failure in one area can quickly spread, creating systemic risk. This was evident in 2008 when the failure of Lehman Brothers, a single investment bank, sent shockwaves through global markets, affecting industries and economies far removed from Wall Street.

Recovery from such crises is never easy or quick. Governments and central banks often step in with recovery strategies, such as bailouts, stimulus packages, and monetary easing, to stabilize the economy. In 2008, the U.S. government introduced the Troubled Asset Relief Program (TARP), injecting billions of dollars into failing banks to prevent a total collapse. While controversial, these measures helped restore confidence and kickstart the recovery process.

Still, the scars of a crisis linger, shaping public perception and policy for years to come.

These cycles of boom and bust are not confined to modern economies. Historical examples, like the Great Depression of the 1930s or the South Sea Bubble of the 18th century, show that the factors driving financial collapses, speculation, lack of oversight, and systemic risk, are remarkably consistent. Despite advances in technology and regulatory frameworks, human behavior remains a constant, often repeating the same mistakes in different forms.

Ripple Effect

The consequences of banking crises extend far beyond the financial sector. Families lose homes, businesses shut down, and governments face mounting debt. The ripple effects touch every corner of society, eroding trust in institutions and deepening economic inequality. Yet, crises also serve as catalysts for change. The 2008 crisis, for instance, led to significant regulatory reforms, such as the Dodd-Frank Act in the U.S., aimed at increasing transparency and reducing risk in the financial system.

Even with safeguards in place, the risk of future crises remains.

Economic cycles are, after all, a natural part of the system. The challenge lies in mitigating their severity and minimizing the harm they cause. For individuals, this might mean making prudent financial choices, like diversifying investments and maintaining savings. For banks, it means adhering to rigorous risk management practices and maintaining sufficient reserves. For governments and central banks, it means finding the right balance between intervention and allowing markets to self-correct.

Conclusion: Key Takeaways and Insights

The lessons of past crises are invaluable, serving as guideposts for navigating future challenges, but they're not always enough to prevent the next one. Economic cycles, human behavior, and unforeseen circumstances often lead to new challenges that test the resilience of financial systems. Crises like the 2008 financial collapse or the debt crises in emerging markets have taught us much about systemic vulnerabilities, the importance of regulation, and the need for trust in institutions. Yet, history shows that while we can prepare for familiar patterns, unexpected risks often emerge from areas we least anticipate. This makes vigilance and adaptability crucial as we look ahead.

As we move forward, understanding the interconnectedness of global economies becomes increasingly vital.

In our modern world, money flows freely, driven by trade, investments, and international markets, creating opportunities for growth but also amplifying risks. A financial decision in one part of the world, whether it's a central bank policy change or a major investment shift, can send ripples across continents. For instance, a currency devaluation in one country can impact trade balances globally, affecting industries and economies far removed from the initial event.

This interconnectedness highlights the need to view money not just as a local or national concern but as a global force. Understanding how money flows between nations helps us grasp the complexities of trade, currencies, and economic relationships. From foreign exchange markets to trade deficits, these dynamics influence not only governments and corporations but also the lives of everyday people. Exchange rates can affect the cost of imported goods, international travel, or even a business's ability to compete in the global market.

As we delve deeper, we'll explore the forces that shape the movement of money across nations, uncovering the intricate balance between trade policies, currency valuations, and economic power.

This brings us to the next chapter, where we'll investigate the global flow of money and its far-reaching impact.

How do countries manage trade imbalances, and what role do currencies play in economic dominance? What happens when globalization connects economies in ways that amplify both opportunities and vulnerabilities?

The answers to these questions reveal the fragile yet dynamic nature of our interconnected world. By understanding the complexities of global money, we can better navigate the opportunities and challenges that come with living in an economy where borders matter less, but interdependence matters more.

Have you ever wondered how the flow of money across the globe shapes the fate of nations and the lives of millions? In the next chapter, we'll uncover the fascinating dynamics of global money and explore its profound impact on how economies operate and thrive. What hidden forces drive international finance, and how do these movements create opportunities or challenges in an interconnected world?

By diving into this intricate web of global connections, you'll gain a deeper appreciation for the power of money to influence the course of history. Get ready to be inspired by the incredible story of how money moves the world!

CHAPTER 6: Global Money: Trade, Exchange, and Power

Money has a way of ignoring borders. It flows seamlessly from one nation to another, crossing oceans and continents to shape the global economy. This movement connects industries, fuels growth, and, at times, sparks conflicts. At its heart, the international flow of money revolves around trade, foreign exchange, and the balance of economic power.

How Money Moves

From the food we eat to the gadgets we use, much of what we consume relies on this vast and intricate web of global financial interactions. Yet, understanding how money moves between nations is as important as understanding how it circulates within them.

Trade is the backbone of the global economy, and money is its lifeblood. When a country exports goods, it earns money from other nations, strengthening its economy. Conversely, importing goods sends money abroad, enriching foreign producers. Ideally, trade creates mutual benefits, but imbalances often arise. A trade deficit, for example, occurs when a country imports more than it exports. The United States has long run significant trade deficits, relying on foreign goods while sending dollars to nations like China. These imbalances can lead to tension, especially when one side feels disadvantaged or overly dependent.

Currency Valuation

Currency valuation plays a crucial role in trade dynamics. Exchange rates determine how much one currency is worth compared to another, influencing trade and investment decisions. A strong currency makes imports cheaper but can hurt exporters by making their goods more expensive abroad. Conversely, a weaker currency boosts exports but increases the cost of imports. Nations often walk a fine line, trying to maintain a currency value that supports economic stability while remaining competitive in global markets.

Central banks sometimes intervene in currency markets to achieve these goals, tying this chapter back to their role as economic regulators.

The foreign exchange market is where currencies are traded, and its size is staggering.

Trillions of dollars move through this market daily, as businesses, governments, and investors exchange currencies for trade, travel, and investment. A multinational company selling cars in Europe might convert euros into dollars, while a tourist visiting Japan exchanges dollars for yen. These seemingly small transactions, when aggregated, have a profound impact on the global economy, shaping everything from interest rates to commodity prices.

Globalization

Globalization has amplified the flow of money and its influence. Over the last few decades, advances in technology and communication have created a world where goods, services, and capital move faster than ever. Companies outsource production to countries with lower labor costs, while consumers benefit from a wider array of products. However, globalization also brings challenges. It has widened economic inequality in some regions, as jobs shift from one country to another.

It has also made economies more interconnected, meaning that a financial crisis in one nation can quickly spread to others, as we saw during the 2008 financial meltdown.

Economic power is deeply tied to global money flows. Nations with strong economies and currencies often wield significant influence on the world stage. The U.S. dollar, for example, is the world's dominant reserve currency, used in international trade and held by central banks worldwide. This status gives the United States a unique advantage, allowing it to borrow cheaply and exert financial influence over other nations. However, this power isn't absolute. Emerging economies like China and India are increasingly challenging the traditional hierarchy, reshaping the balance of global economic power.

Trade agreements and international institutions also play a role in managing global money flows.

Organizations like the World Trade Organization (WTO) and the International Monetary Fund (IMF) work to facilitate trade, resolve disputes, and promote economic stability. These frameworks help maintain order in an otherwise chaotic system, ensuring that countries can engage in trade fairly and efficiently. But they are not without criticism, as some argue they favor wealthier nations at the expense of developing ones.

Despite its complexities, the global flow of money brings undeniable benefits. It fosters cooperation, innovation, and economic growth, enabling nations to specialize in what they do best. A country rich in natural resources can trade them for advanced technology, while a nation with a skilled workforce can export high-quality services. This interconnectedness creates opportunities but also vulnerabilities, as no economy operates in isolation.

Conclusion: Key Takeaways and Insights

Global money flows are not just about transactions or trade; they are about power, who controls it, who benefits from it, and who is left behind.

Understanding these dynamics is essential for navigating the complexities of the modern world.

Whether it's a farmer in Brazil exporting coffee, a tech startup in Silicon Valley seeking international investment, or a consumer in France buying goods from Japan, the interconnected nature of these relationships defines economies and shapes lives. Money isn't just a medium of exchange; it's a force that determines influence, drives decisions, and, at times, exacerbates inequalities.

This flow of global money rewards efficiency but ruthlessly punishes imbalance.

Countries with strong economies, innovative industries, and stable currencies often hold a disproportionate share of power, leveraging their financial systems to shape international trade and policy. Meanwhile, nations with weaker economies or unstable currencies can find themselves at the mercy of global markets, their decisions constrained by external forces beyond their control. This uneven distribution of power is a hallmark of the global economy, reflecting historical legacies and contemporary realities.

The system is constantly evolving, adapting to reflect the shifting dynamics of a changing world.

Trade agreements, geopolitical tensions, and economic alliances all play a role in determining how money moves and who benefits. A country that invests in technological innovation or sustainable practices can gain a competitive edge, enhancing its economic standing. Conversely, those that fail to adapt risk falling behind, their influence diminishing in an increasingly interconnected system.

As we move forward, the role of technology in this global system becomes increasingly significant.

Innovations like cryptocurrencies, blockchain, and digital payment platforms are not only changing how money flows but also challenging traditional power structures. Cryptocurrencies, for example, bypass traditional financial institutions, offering the promise of greater financial freedom but also raising concerns about regulation and stability. Blockchain technology introduces transparency and decentralization, potentially shifting power away from centralized authorities toward a more distributed model.

These technological advancements carry promises and challenges in equal measure. On the one hand, they could democratize access to financial systems, empowering individuals and nations previously excluded from traditional banking and investment opportunities. On the other hand, they also present risks, such as the potential for misuse, cybersecurity threats, and the destabilization of established economic frameworks. The balance of power in the global economy could be profoundly affected by how these technologies are adopted, regulated, and integrated into existing systems.

In the next chapter, we'll dive deeper into this technological revolution reshaping money and banking.

We'll explore how innovations like blockchain and digital currencies are influencing the flow of money, challenging the status quo, and redefining power in the financial landscape. By understanding these developments, we can better anticipate the opportunities and risks that lie ahead in this ever-evolving system.

CHAPTER 7: The Technology Revolution: Digital Currencies and Beyond

The world of money is no stranger to change, but the pace of innovation in recent years has been staggering. Technology has not just nudged banking and finance forward; it has catapulted them into a new era.

Accessibility and Convenience

Gone are the days when visiting a bank branch was the only way to handle money. Today, transactions happen in seconds, often without the need for physical cash. From digital banking and online payments to cryptocurrencies and decentralized finance, technology is rewriting the rules of the financial world, creating opportunities and challenges we've never seen before.

Think about how easy it is now to send money to someone halfway across the world.

With a few taps on your phone, you can transfer funds instantly, bypassing the delays and fees that traditional banking systems once imposed. Apps like

PayPal, Venmo, and others have become household names, making peer-to-peer payments seamless. This shift isn't just about convenience, it's about accessibility. People who once lacked access to traditional banking services now use mobile apps to save, borrow, and invest, bridging gaps that seemed insurmountable just a decade ago.

Blockchain

One of the most transformative innovations in recent history is blockchain technology. At its core, a blockchain is a decentralized ledger that records transactions across a network of computers.

Unlike traditional banking systems that rely on a central authority to verify transactions, blockchain is maintained by a community of users. This eliminates the need for intermediaries, reducing costs and increasing transparency. It's the backbone of cryptocurrencies like Bitcoin and Ethereum, but its potential extends far beyond digital money. From supply chain management to secure voting systems, blockchain is being hailed as a game-changer across industries.

Cryptocurrencies

Cryptocurrencies are perhaps the most talked-about application of blockchain. Bitcoin, the first cryptocurrency, emerged in 2009, introducing the world to the idea of decentralized digital money.

Unlike fiat currencies, Bitcoin isn't controlled by any government or central bank. Instead, it operates on a peer-to-peer network, where transactions are verified and recorded on the blockchain. Over time, thousands of other cryptocurrencies have been created, each with its unique features and use cases.

Ethereum, for example, enables smart contracts, self-executing agreements coded into the blockchain, unlocking new possibilities for automation and efficiency.

Yet, cryptocurrencies remain a polarizing topic.

Advocates tout their potential to disrupt traditional finance, offering greater privacy, security, and financial inclusion. Critics, however, point to their volatility, energy consumption, and potential for misuse. Bitcoin's price, for instance, has swung wildly over the years, making it more of a speculative asset than a stable currency for daily transactions.

Governments and regulators are grappling with how to address these challenges, striking a balance between encouraging innovation and protecting consumers.

Decentralized Finance

Decentralized finance, or DeFi, takes the ideas behind cryptocurrencies a step further. DeFi platforms aim to replicate traditional financial services, like lending, borrowing, and trading, without the need for banks or intermediaries. Instead, they use smart contracts to automate these processes, making them faster, cheaper, and more accessible. Imagine earning interest on your savings without ever stepping foot in a bank or obtaining a loan without a lengthy approval process.

DeFi is still in its infancy, but its potential to democratize finance is immense, particularly in regions where banking infrastructure is underdeveloped.

Fintech

Traditional banks haven't ignored these trends. Many are embracing technology to stay competitive, investing in fintech solutions and partnering with startups to modernize their services. Digital banking has become the norm, with apps offering features like budgeting tools, instant transfers, and even AI-driven financial advice. These innovations cater to a tech-savvy generation that expects convenience and personalization in every aspect of their lives. At the same time, banks face increasing competition from fintech companies and digital-native financial platforms that are reshaping customer expectations. But with innovation comes risk.

Conclusion: Key Takeaways and Insights

The rise of digital currencies and decentralized systems introduces new challenges that financial systems are only beginning to grapple with.

Cybersecurity threats loom large in this digital age, with hackers constantly seeking vulnerabilities in digital wallets and online platforms. Even the most secure systems are not immune to breaches, as evidenced by numerous high-profile cyberattacks on cryptocurrency exchanges and financial institutions. The very attributes that make cryptocurrencies attractive, decentralization, anonymity, and lack of central control, also make them ideal for misuse in illicit activities, from money laundering to funding illegal enterprises.

These risks have prompted growing calls for stricter oversight and regulation, but finding the right balance between fostering innovation and ensuring security remains a delicate task.

Blockchain technology, the foundation of cryptocurrencies, is central to this conversation.

At its core, blockchain is a decentralized ledger that records transactions across a network of computers. Its design makes it highly secure and transparent, as each transaction is verified by the network and permanently recorded. This eliminates the need for intermediaries, reducing costs and increasing efficiency. Beyond cryptocurrencies like Bitcoin and Ethereum, blockchain's potential applications extend to fields as diverse as supply chain management, healthcare, and even voting systems. By offering a tamper-proof way to track and verify information, blockchain has the potential to transform industries far beyond finance.

However, the adoption of blockchain also raises questions about power and control. Decentralized systems challenge traditional financial institutions by removing their gatekeeping role. In a blockchain-based economy, individuals and businesses could theoretically transact directly with one another without relying on banks or payment processors. This could democratize access to financial systems, particularly in regions where traditional banking infrastructure is limited. Yet, this very decentralization also makes regulation difficult, as no single entity controls the system.

Governments and regulators are faced with the challenge of adapting existing laws to a technology that operates outside traditional frameworks.

Despite these challenges, the benefits of financial technology cannot be overstated. Digital platforms have made banking more inclusive, offering services to billions of people who previously lacked access to financial systems. Mobile banking, online payments, and peer-to-peer lending platforms have empowered individuals in underserved regions, giving them tools to save, invest, and build businesses. Blockchain-based systems could take this even further by creating a global financial network that transcends borders, offering opportunities to those who have been left behind by traditional systems.

Technology has also redefined what we expect from financial institutions.

Banks, once seen as slow-moving and bureaucratic, are now competing with agile fintech startups that prioritize user experience, speed, and transparency. This competition has pushed traditional institutions to innovate, adopting technologies like artificial intelligence and machine learning to enhance services and improve efficiency. The ripple effects of this revolution are reshaping global trade, investment strategies, and individual financial decisions, ensuring that no aspect of the financial system remains untouched.

As we look ahead, the future of money feels more uncertain yet more exciting than ever.

Will cryptocurrencies eventually replace traditional currencies, or will they coexist in a hybrid system where both play complementary roles? How will governments and regulators adapt to an increasingly decentralized financial world, where control is distributed among networks rather than centralized authorities? And how will new technologies, like quantum computing, impact the security and scalability of blockchain-based systems? These questions remain unanswered, but they hint at a future that is as complex as it is transformative.

The financial landscape is on the cusp of unprecedented change, driven by the twin forces of innovation and adaptability.

Trust, a recurring theme throughout the evolution of money, will be pivotal in shaping this future. Whether it's trust in new technologies, trust in institutions to manage them responsibly, or trust among individuals to navigate this changing world, it will form the bedrock of the next chapter in the story of money.

What does the future hold for money and banking in a world that's changing faster than ever? Next, we'll embark on a journey to uncover the possibilities, challenges, and breakthroughs that lie ahead. From the complexities of regulation to the exciting promises of inclusivity and efficiency, we'll explore how trust, innovation, and adaptability are poised to reshape economies, societies, and even the very concept of value itself. How will these changes impact the way we live, work, and interact with the world around us?

Get ready to dive into this rapidly evolving landscape and discover the forces that are redefining the future of finance. The possibilities may surprise you!

CHAPTER 8: The Future of Money and Banking: Trust, Innovation, and Change

The story of money and banking is far from over. If anything, we're standing at the threshold of another profound transformation, one that will redefine how economies operate and how people interact with money. The rapid pace of technological innovation and the shifting priorities of societies are reshaping the financial landscape.

Faster and Cheaper

Trust remains the cornerstone of this system, but the ways in which it is earned and maintained are evolving. As we look to the future, themes like adaptability, sustainability, and inclusivity take center stage, offering a glimpse of what lies ahead.

One of the most obvious changes on the horizon is the continued rise of financial technology.

Fintech has already disrupted traditional banking by offering faster, cheaper, and more accessible solutions, but this is just the beginning. Imagine a world where artificial intelligence provides personalized financial advice tailored to your unique goals, or where blockchain technology eliminates inefficiencies in international trade. These innovations promise to make the financial system not only more efficient but also more equitable, as people in underserved regions gain access to tools that were once out of reach.

Sustainability

Sustainability is another key factor shaping the future of money and banking. Banks are increasingly expected to align their practices with environmental and social goals, supporting investments in renewable energy and sustainable industries.

This shift reflects a growing recognition that economic growth must go hand in hand with protecting the planet.

The rise of green bonds and other sustainable financial instruments illustrates how markets are adapting to these demands. Central banks, too, are exploring how monetary policy can address climate risks, signaling a broader transformation in how financial systems operate.

Trust

Yet, no matter how advanced technology becomes, the importance of trust cannot be overstated. People need to believe that their money is safe, their transactions are secure, and their financial institutions are acting in their best interests.

This trust is being tested in new ways as cyber threats grow more sophisticated and decentralized systems challenge traditional oversight mechanisms. Striking a balance between innovation and security will be critical in maintaining public confidence as the financial landscape evolves.

Adaptability

The adaptability of institutions and individuals will also play a significant role in shaping the future. History has shown that those who embrace change thrive, while those who resist it risk being left behind. Traditional banks that once saw fintech as a threat are now partnering with startups to enhance their services. Similarly, individuals who learn to navigate new financial tools, such as digital currencies or investment platforms, are better positioned to take advantage of emerging opportunities. Flexibility and a willingness to learn will be invaluable in this rapidly changing environment.

Societal Values

Economic transformation is not limited to technology. Societal values are shifting, influencing how money is viewed and used. Younger generations, for example, are prioritizing experiences over material possessions and seeking financial products that align with their ethical beliefs. This change in consumer behavior is prompting businesses and banks to rethink their offerings, emphasizing transparency, sustainability, and social impact.

These trends are reshaping markets, creating new opportunities, and challenging old norms.

Globalization

Globalization and interconnectedness add yet another layer of complexity to this ever-evolving financial landscape. As money moves seamlessly across borders, driven by trade, investment, and innovation, the need for international cooperation and effective regulation grows more urgent. A decision made by a central bank in one country can ripple across global markets, influencing currencies, trade balances, and even the policies of other nations. Cryptocurrencies and decentralized finance have introduced entirely new dimensions to this equation, challenging governments to rethink regulatory frameworks and address the unique risks and opportunities posed by these technologies.

Global trade continues to depend on the stability of financial systems to ensure smooth transactions and predictable outcomes.

Disruptions in one part of the world, such as a banking crisis or currency devaluation, can quickly spread, highlighting the delicate balance required to maintain economic stability. The role of central banks, already a cornerstone of national economies, will remain crucial in navigating these challenges. These institutions must strike a careful balance between fostering innovation, managing risks, and maintaining public trust.

Central banks are not only guardians of monetary stability but also key players in the global economy's ability to adapt to rapid changes.

Their decisions on interest rates, money supply, and financial oversight will shape how economies respond to the pressures of globalization, technological advancement, and unforeseen crises. In a world that is more connected than ever, their ability to navigate these complexities is essential to ensuring the global economy stays on course and thrives amidst rapid transformation.

Conclusion: Key Takeaways and Insights

While the road ahead is uncertain, it is also full of potential. The future of money and banking will likely be shaped by the delicate interplay of trust, innovation, and adaptability. These forces will determine how financial systems evolve, who benefits from them, and how they address the challenges of a changing world. The ability to balance progress with stability, inclusivity with efficiency, and ambition with caution will shape not only the financial system but also the society we live in.

Every decision made, whether by individuals, businesses, or governments, has a role in steering this evolution, reinforcing the importance of understanding the interconnected nature of money and its impact on the world.

Understanding these systems goes beyond institutions, policies, and markets.

At its core, money is deeply personal, and how we interact with it reflects our values, emotions, and circumstances. This is why the next chapter delves into *The Psychology of Money: Why We Spend, Save, and Invest*. Our financial choices often stem from far more than logic, they are influenced by emotions, biases, habits, and the subtle ways we perceive risk and reward. Exploring these psychological dimensions helps illuminate the human element that underpins the seemingly impersonal structures of banking and economics.

When people make decisions to save, spend, or invest, they are not only shaping their personal financial futures but also contributing to broader economic trends. The tendency to save during uncertain times or spend impulsively during periods of confidence ripples through markets and institutions, driving cycles of growth and contraction. Banks, businesses, and governments respond to these patterns, adjusting policies and strategies to align with consumer behavior. By examining these patterns, the next chapter reveals the intricate dance between individual psychology and the larger financial ecosystem.

This exploration also highlights why understanding our own financial behaviors is essential. Awareness of how emotions and biases influence our decisions allows us to make more informed choices. Whether it's avoiding the pitfalls of impulsive spending, developing consistent saving habits, or approaching investments with a rational mindset, financial literacy rooted in psychological insight can empower individuals to navigate the complexities of money more effectively.

Have you ever considered how your personal financial choices are connected to the larger forces that drive economies and shape the world of money and banking? As we continue this journey, the next chapter will reveal the profound link between personal finance and broader economic forces, showing how every decision, big or small, contributes to the greater financial narrative. What role do you play in this interconnected system, and how can understanding it empower you to make smarter choices?

By exploring the human side of these vast systems, you'll uncover practical insights and gain a deeper appreciation of the impact we all have in shaping financial realities. Get ready to see your place in the world of money like never before!

CHAPTER 9: The Psychology of Money: Why We Spend, Save, and Invest

Money has always been more than just a tool; it's deeply personal. While numbers and calculations play a role, our relationship with money is driven by emotions, habits, and psychology. Why do some people save diligently while others can't resist spending on the latest gadget? Why does investing feel exciting to some but nerve-wracking to others?

Behavioral Economics

Behavioral economics explores these questions, revealing how our minds shape financial decisions, and often, how these decisions defy logic.

Think about the last time you made a significant financial choice. Maybe it was a splurge on a vacation or a moment of hesitation before investing in the stock market. Did your decision feel entirely rational, or did emotions creep in? Perhaps you were motivated by the joy of experiencing something new, or maybe fear of losing money held you back. Emotions like fear, excitement, and even guilt can heavily influence how we spend, save, and invest, sometimes leading to decisions that feel right in the moment but hurt us later.

Cognitive Biases

Cognitive biases are a key part of this story. These mental shortcuts, while useful in some situations, often steer us away from sound financial choices.

Loss aversion is a prime example. People fear losing money more than they value gaining it, which can make them overly cautious. This is why some avoid investing in stocks, even when long-term returns are promising. Another common bias is the anchoring effect, where initial impressions distort decision-making. For instance, if an item is marked "50% off," we're more likely to buy it, even if we don't actually need it, because our mind fixates on the discount rather than the actual value.

These biases don't just affect spending; they also influence saving habits. Saving requires discipline and a long-term perspective, qualities that don't always come naturally. For many, the immediate gratification of spending outweighs the abstract benefits of saving for the future. Tools like automatic savings plans and budgeting apps help by tapping into behavioral insights, making the process easier and less reliant on willpower. These strategies have reshaped how individuals approach saving, blending psychology with practical tools to encourage better habits.

Investing, too, is fraught with psychological hurdles. Risk perception plays a significant role in whether someone invests or stays on the sidelines.

During a market downturn, fear often drives people to sell their investments prematurely, locking in losses. Conversely, during a bull market, overconfidence can lead to reckless decisions, like chasing high-flying stocks without considering their true value. Behavioral finance has shown that understanding these patterns can help investors develop more rational strategies, focusing on long-term goals rather than short-term emotions.

Banks and financial institutions are not immune to these psychological influences. In fact, they've become adept at leveraging them. Credit card rewards programs, for example, tap into our desire for instant gratification, encouraging spending by offering points or cash back. Limited-time offers and promotional interest rates capitalize on our fear of missing out, driving decisions that might not align with our financial priorities. Understanding how psychology interacts with financial products can empower individuals to make more informed choices and avoid falling into traps designed to exploit their biases.

The ripple effects of financial psychology extend to entire economies.

Consumer behavior drives demand, influencing markets and shaping economic growth. During times of economic uncertainty, like recessions, fear often leads to widespread saving, reducing spending and slowing the economy. On the flip side, overconfidence during booms can create financial bubbles, as we discussed in the chapter on banking crises. These cycles, driven by collective psychology, highlight the profound impact emotions have on markets and economies.

Financial Literacy

Financial literacy is key to navigating these challenges. By understanding the emotional and psychological factors that drive financial decisions, individuals can develop better habits and avoid common pitfalls. Simple steps, like setting clear financial goals or seeking advice from trusted experts, can make a significant difference. Similarly, banks and governments have a role to play in fostering financial literacy, creating systems that support sound decision-making rather than preying on vulnerabilities.

The intersection of psychology, money, and banking underscores the importance of trust, a theme woven throughout this book. Trust in oneself to make wise choices, trust in institutions to act responsibly, and trust in the broader economic system are all crucial for financial stability. As we've seen, the relationship between money and psychology is complex, but it's also deeply human.

Conclusion: Key Takeaways and Insights

This chapter serves as a reminder that while money may be a product of systems and institutions, it is also profoundly shaped by the choices, habits, and emotions of the people who use it.

Money, at its core, is a reflection of human behavior, our aspirations, fears, and desires, and understanding these psychological forces is crucial to navigating the financial world.

Why we spend, save, or invest is often less about logic and more about how we perceive value, manage risk, and respond to external pressures. These decisions ripple through economies, influencing markets and shaping the broader financial landscape.

Spending, for example, is not always a simple exchange of money for goods or services; it's often an emotional act. We might spend to reward ourselves, to signal success to others, or even as a coping mechanism during difficult times. Retail therapy is a real phenomenon, rooted in the temporary boost of happiness we feel when purchasing something new. But overspending, especially on credit, can lead to financial stress and debt, creating long-term problems from short-term emotional decisions. By recognizing these patterns, we can take steps to align our spending with our goals, rather than letting emotions dictate our choices.

Saving, on the other hand, often requires the opposite approach, delayed gratification.

While spending feels immediate and tangible, saving is about planning for a future that can sometimes feel distant or uncertain. The psychology of saving is deeply tied to individual mindset and cultural influences. For some, saving comes naturally, driven by a sense of security or fear of the unknown. For others, it can feel restrictive, even unnecessary, especially in the absence of clear goals. Tools like automated savings apps and gamified financial platforms have emerged to make saving easier and more engaging, tapping into behavioral insights to encourage positive habits.

Investing introduces yet another layer of complexity, blending psychology with strategy.

Risk perception plays a significant role in determining whether someone invests and how they approach it. Fear of loss can cause people to shy away from investments altogether, even when potential rewards outweigh the risks. Conversely, overconfidence can lead others to take unnecessary risks, chasing high returns without fully understanding the market. Behavioral finance has revealed countless biases that influence investment decisions, from the tendency to follow the crowd during market booms to the reluctance to cut losses when an investment underperforms. Awareness of these biases can help individuals make more rational, informed choices.

The human element in finance, however, is a double-edged sword.

Just as psychology can drive responsible financial behavior, it can also pave the way for misconduct, greed, and unethical practices. History is rife with examples of financial collapses driven by poor decisions or outright fraud, from speculative bubbles to corporate scandals. The emotions and biases that influence individual behavior also manifest on a larger scale, affecting institutions and markets. When fear, greed, or overconfidence take hold, the consequences can be disastrous, eroding trust and destabilizing economies.

By becoming more aware of these psychological forces, we can approach the financial world with greater clarity and make decisions that align with our goals and values. Financial literacy, rooted in an understanding of both practical concepts and emotional drivers, is key to navigating the complexities of money. It's not just about knowing how to budget or invest, it's about recognizing the emotions and biases that influence those decisions.

Self-awareness enables individuals to build healthier financial habits and avoid common pitfalls.

As we reflect on the journey through money and banking, it's crucial to recognize the opportunities for growth, stability, and innovation that lie ahead. The intersection of psychology and finance offers insights into how individuals and systems interact, revealing ways to foster greater inclusivity and resilience. Yet, alongside these opportunities are significant risks. The same human behaviors that drive progress can also lead to misconduct and systemic vulnerabilities.

What happens when the very systems we rely on for stability and growth are shaken by scandals and corruption? In the next chapter, we'll venture into the darker side of money and banking, uncovering the high-profile failures and systemic weaknesses that have sent shockwaves through economies and societies. How do these events expose the fragility of trust, and what lessons can we learn to prevent them in the future?

By exploring these cautionary tales, you'll gain a deeper appreciation for the critical role transparency, accountability, and robust regulations play in creating a financial system that works for everyone. This journey into the shadows will also reveal the ongoing fight to safeguard integrity in an increasingly interconnected and complex world. Get ready to uncover the truths that lie beneath the surface!

CHAPTER 10: The Dark Side of Money and Banking: Scandals, Corruption, and Crime

Money may be the lifeblood of the economy, but it has a shadowy side that has caused its fair share of harm. Scandals, corruption, and crime are unfortunate realities in the world of banking and finance, arising wherever there's a concentration of power and wealth.

These issues expose vulnerabilities in financial systems and test the trust upon which economies depend. While regulation and oversight have evolved to address these challenges, history has shown that bad actors often stay one step ahead, exploiting gaps in systems designed to ensure fairness and stability.

Libor Scandal

One of the most glaring examples of banking misconduct is the LIBOR scandal. For years, major financial institutions manipulated the London Interbank Offered Rate (LIBOR), a benchmark that influenced interest rates worldwide. By inflating or deflating the rate for their gain, these banks impacted everything from mortgages to student loans, affecting millions of people. When the scandal came to light, the public's trust in banks was shaken, and regulators scrambled to implement stricter controls. It was a sobering reminder that even the most sophisticated systems can be undermined by unethical practices.

HSBC

Money laundering is another dark corner of the financial world. Criminal enterprises often use banks to "clean" illicit money, making it appear legitimate. The scale of these operations is staggering, involving billions of dollars annually. In one infamous case, HSBC was fined nearly $2 billion after it was revealed that the bank had facilitated transactions for drug cartels and other criminal organizations. These revelations exposed weaknesses in compliance systems, raising questions about how effectively banks monitor transactions and enforce anti-money laundering regulations.

Nick Leeson and Barings Bank

Scandals aren't limited to large institutions; they also occur at the individual level. Rogue traders, like Nick Leeson, whose unauthorized trading brought down Barings Bank in the 1990s, demonstrate how a single person's actions can destabilize an entire organization. Such cases often highlight a failure of oversight, where internal systems are either too weak or too easily bypassed. The ripple effects of these actions can extend far beyond the bank itself, impacting shareholders, employees, and the broader economy.

Systemic Risk

Systemic risks posed by these scandals are enormous. When trust in financial institutions falters, it can trigger a chain reaction of withdrawals, reduced lending, and economic contraction. This was evident during the global financial crisis of 2008, where excessive risk-taking and opaque practices led to widespread banking collapses. Governments were forced to intervene with massive bailouts, further straining public trust in the financial system. These crises underscore the importance of transparency and accountability in maintaining stability.

Regulation is critical in addressing these challenges, but it's often reactive rather than proactive. Scandals expose weaknesses in existing frameworks, prompting new laws and policies. Anti-money laundering (AML) laws, for instance, have grown more robust over time, requiring banks to verify customer identities and monitor suspicious transactions. However, no regulatory system is foolproof. Criminals adapt quickly, finding new ways to exploit financial networks, particularly as technology evolves.

Trust is the glue that holds financial systems together, and rebuilding it after a scandal is no easy task.

Institutions must show that they've learned from past mistakes, implementing stronger controls and prioritizing ethical behavior. Transparency plays a crucial role in this process. By openly addressing misconduct and demonstrating accountability, banks can begin to restore public confidence. The challenge lies in balancing these efforts with the need to remain competitive in a fast-paced, profit-driven environment.

Conclusion: Key Takeaways and Insights

While scandals and corruption paint a grim picture, they also serve as catalysts for progress. Each failure brings valuable lessons that help reshape the future of money and banking.

How do we ensure that tighter regulations are not just reactive measures but proactive frameworks that anticipate new risks? Can advanced compliance technologies, powered by artificial intelligence and machine learning, outpace the creative strategies of those who seek to exploit the system? What does fostering a culture of ethics look like in practice, and how do financial institutions balance profitability with responsibility? These efforts aim not only to prevent misconduct but also to rebuild and reinforce the trust that is so essential to the stability of the global economy.

Understanding the dark side of money and banking serves as a reminder of the fragility of financial systems and the vigilance required to protect them.

If trust is the foundation of these systems, how do we rebuild it after it's been shaken? Is transparency enough to restore public confidence, or do institutions need to do more to demonstrate accountability? What role do individuals play in holding these systems accountable, and how can governments ensure that their regulations are effective without stifling innovation? These are the critical questions that emerge as we reflect on past failures and look toward a future where trust must be earned repeatedly, not assumed.

As we look to the future, the lessons of the past offer invaluable guidance.

How do we balance the rapid pace of innovation with the slower processes of regulatory oversight? Can progress and integrity coexist in a financial world driven by competition and profit? What mechanisms can be put in place to ensure that the mistakes of the past are not repeated, and that emerging risks are identified before they escalate? Ensuring that innovation and progress are built on a foundation of integrity is not just a challenge for financial institutions but a shared responsibility that spans governments, businesses, and individuals.

Equally important is preparing for the inevitable storms that test these systems.

Financial crises, whether global or local, have taught us that resilience is not a luxury but a necessity. How can individuals safeguard their savings and investments against unforeseen economic shocks?

What strategies can businesses adopt to remain agile and adaptable during times of uncertainty? How can governments strike the right balance between intervention and allowing market forces to play out? These questions become even more pressing as we navigate a world where interconnectedness amplifies both opportunities and vulnerabilities.

In the next chapter, we'll explore how individuals, businesses, and governments can build financial resilience to adapt and recover when challenges arise.

Have you ever wondered what it takes to build financial systems that can withstand the storms of uncertainty and emerge even stronger? What tools and strategies can fortify economies at every level, ensuring resilience and growth?

In the next chapter, we'll uncover the lessons learned from past crises and explore how these insights can shape future policies and practices.

Most importantly, we'll address the critical question: How can trust be preserved during periods of instability, keeping financial systems as the pillars of progress and stability we all rely on? Join us as we dive into the strategies and mindsets that empower individuals, businesses, and nations to navigate economic challenges and thrive in a rapidly evolving world. You won't want to miss what's next!

CHAPTER 11: How to Weather Economic Storms

Economic storms come in many forms. Sometimes they manifest as a sudden recession that disrupts markets and livelihoods; other times, they arise as personal financial crises, like losing a job or facing unexpected expenses.

On a larger scale, global events such as pandemics can ripple across the world, destabilising economies and leaving individuals, businesses, and governments scrambling to recover. These disruptions, whether personal or systemic, test the stability of financial systems and highlight vulnerabilities that may have gone unnoticed during periods of prosperity.

While the challenges presented by these economic shocks can feel overwhelming, resilience offers a way forward, a beacon of hope amidst uncertainty.

Financial resilience is far more than just the ability to endure tough times; it is the capacity to adapt, recover, and thrive despite the odds. It involves not only weathering the storm but also taking proactive steps to prepare for future uncertainties, responding strategically in the moment, and learning valuable lessons from adversity.

Building financial resilience is a multifaceted journey. It encompasses strengthening personal financial habits, such as saving, budgeting, and reducing debt, to creating robust strategies at the organisational and governmental levels. It's about anticipating risks, recognising warning signs, and implementing measures that minimise damage when crises arise. More importantly, it's about fostering a mindset that views challenges as opportunities for growth and innovation.

As we explore the concept of financial resilience, we'll uncover practical tools and strategies that enable individuals, businesses, and nations to navigate economic shocks with confidence. By understanding how to prepare effectively, respond decisively, and emerge stronger, we can not only survive disruptions but also use them as a foundation for a more secure and prosperous future. Resilience is not just about surviving; it's about thriving in a world of uncertainty, and that journey begins now.

Emergency Fund

For individuals, financial resilience often starts with one fundamental step: establishing an emergency fund. This financial safety net serves as a crucial buffer against unexpected expenses, such as medical bills, car repairs, or even the sudden loss of income due to job loss.

Without a cushion, these unforeseen events can quickly escalate into significant financial crises, creating a cascade of stress and debt that can be difficult to recover from.

Experts generally recommend setting aside three to six months' worth of living expenses to cover essentials like housing, utilities, and food. While this might seem like an intimidating goal, it's important to remember that building an emergency fund is not an all-or-nothing proposition. Even saving smaller amounts over time can provide a meaningful level of protection and make a tangible difference in managing financial shocks.

The key lies in consistency, small, regular contributions add up, gradually creating a layer of security that can help mitigate immediate stress during tough times.

Establishing an emergency fund also ties back to broader financial habits discussed earlier, such as prioritising savings and maintaining a budget. These habits not only make it easier to build the fund but also encourage a mindset of preparedness and control over one's financial future. It's a process that requires discipline, patience, and a commitment to incremental progress.

Beyond its practical benefits, an emergency fund offers an often-overlooked emotional advantage: peace of mind. Knowing that you have a safety net in place can significantly reduce the anxiety that comes with financial uncertainty. This sense of security fosters greater confidence in making financial decisions, whether it's navigating a short-term setback or planning for long-term goals. An emergency fund is not just a tool for survival, it's a foundation for financial freedom, empowering individuals to face life's uncertainties with greater resilience and optimism.

Diversification

Diversification is another cornerstone of resilience, and it applies to both income sources and investments.

Relying solely on a single source of income or placing all your financial hopes on one type of asset can be a risky gamble. The 2008 financial crisis served as a stark reminder of the dangers of over-concentration, particularly for those heavily invested in real estate. As housing prices plummeted, many saw their wealth tied to property evaporate almost overnight, leaving them financially vulnerable. This hard lesson underscores the importance of diversification, both in investments and income sources, as a key strategy for building resilience.

A diversified portfolio acts as a financial cushion, helping to absorb shocks during market downturns.

By spreading investments across a mix of assets, such as stocks, bonds, savings, real estate, and even alternative investments like commodities, individuals can reduce the risk of significant losses tied to any one sector. Diversification doesn't guarantee immunity from financial turbulence, but it does provide a buffer, ensuring that a decline in one area is less likely to derail an entire financial plan.

Beyond investment diversification, cultivating multiple income streams is another powerful way to enhance financial stability. Side businesses, freelance opportunities, passive income from investments, or even leveraging varied skill sets to take on additional work can create a safety net when primary income sources are disrupted. For example, a part-time consultancy, rental property income, or dividends from stocks can provide much-needed support during periods of job loss or economic instability.

The beauty of having multiple income streams is that it not only reduces reliance on a single employer or market sector but also increases overall financial flexibility and independence.

This approach allows individuals to weather uncertainties more confidently, adapt to changing circumstances, and take advantage of opportunities that might otherwise seem out of reach. Ultimately, diversification, both in investments and income, is not just a hedge against risk; it's a proactive strategy for long-term growth, stability, and peace of mind.

Smart Management

For businesses, financial resilience is a cornerstone of long-term survival and growth, requiring a combination of smart cash flow management, strategic planning, and proactive risk management. Companies that maintain healthy financial reserves and establish robust contingency plans are far better positioned to weather economic slowdowns and unexpected challenges. On the other hand, businesses operating on tight margins, with little room to manoeuvre, often find themselves struggling to stay afloat during crises. Effective cash flow management ensures that businesses can meet their operational needs even in turbulent times, preventing liquidity crunches that can lead to insolvency.

Risk management is another critical aspect of financial resilience.

Businesses must continuously identify and address vulnerabilities in their operations. For example, overreliance on a single supplier, market, or product line can create significant risks, as disruptions in any one of these areas can have a cascading impact on the entire operation. By diversifying suppliers, targeting multiple markets, and expanding product offerings, businesses can spread risk and increase their ability to adapt to changing conditions.

Strategic diversification goes beyond products and markets. Many companies have found that adopting flexible strategies, such as embracing digital transformation or expanding operations geographically, provides additional layers of resilience. Digital transformation, for instance, has enabled businesses to reach broader audiences, streamline operations, and remain competitive in an increasingly online-driven economy. Similarly, geographic expansion can reduce reliance on a single regional market, helping businesses hedge against localized economic downturns or disruptions.

These resilience-building strategies also highlight the interconnectedness of businesses and financial systems, a recurring theme in earlier chapters, particularly in the discussion of banks as vital partners.

Banks play a crucial role in providing credit, liquidity, and financial expertise, which are essential for businesses to navigate challenging times. Companies that cultivate strong relationships with financial institutions and leverage their resources effectively often find themselves better equipped to handle periods of uncertainty.

Ultimately, financial resilience for businesses is not just about surviving crises; it's about thriving in the face of adversity. By proactively managing risks, diversifying operations, and planning strategically, businesses can build the agility and strength needed to capitalize on opportunities, even during turbulent economic times. In doing so, they contribute not only to their own success but also to the stability and growth of the broader financial ecosystem.

Understanding Regulations and Policies

Governments also have a vital role to play in fostering economic resilience. Policies like unemployment benefits, stimulus packages, and targeted support for struggling industries help stabilize economies during downturns. The 2008 financial crisis saw extensive government interventions, including bailouts and quantitative easing, which prevented a deeper collapse. Similarly, during the COVID-19 pandemic, emergency measures protected jobs and businesses worldwide. These actions reinforce the importance of trust in public institutions. Without trust, even well-designed interventions lose effectiveness, as individuals and businesses hesitate to spend, invest, or engage with financial systems.

Systemic risks, such as banking collapses, global cyberattacks, or widespread supply chain disruptions, present another layer of complexity. Addressing these risks requires collaboration between governments, businesses, and individuals. Regulations, such as anti-money laundering laws and transparency requirements, play a critical role in reducing vulnerabilities.

At the same time, advancements in financial technology are offering innovative tools for detecting and mitigating risks. Blockchain, artificial intelligence, and predictive analytics, for example, are being used to create smarter, more adaptive financial systems capable of withstanding systemic shocks.

Adaptability

Adaptability is perhaps the most critical trait of financial resilience. The economic landscape is constantly shifting due to technological advances, geopolitical changes, and global trends. Those who can pivot in response to these changes, whether individuals learning new skills, businesses adjusting to market demands, or governments anticipating challenges like climate change, are better equipped to thrive.

Adaptability also fosters innovation, enabling economies to transform and grow even during times of uncertainty. This idea aligns with earlier chapters exploring the relationship between trust, innovation, and sustainability in financial systems.

Sustainability

Sustainability is increasingly seen as a core component of resilience. Economies built on sustainable practices are inherently more stable, as they reduce dependencies on volatile resources or exploitative practices. Investing in renewable energy, reducing waste, and supporting green initiatives aren't just ethical decisions, they are practical strategies for ensuring long-term economic health. Banks and financial institutions are also embracing this shift, offering green bonds and sustainability-linked loans to encourage responsible growth.

By integrating sustainability into their frameworks, financial systems can create a more equitable and secure future for everyone.

Financial Resilience

Financial resilience isn't a one-size-fits-all solution; it requires a blend of strategies, habits, and mindsets tailored to different circumstances. For individuals, it might mean maintaining an emergency fund and diversifying income streams. For businesses, it could involve building reserves, diversifying operations, and adopting flexible strategies. For governments, resilience means designing policies that protect the most vulnerable while encouraging long-term growth. These principles underscore the importance of preparation, adaptability, and a proactive approach to navigating uncertainty.

As we reflect on these lessons, the importance of trust, innovation, and collaboration comes into sharp focus. Financial resilience is not about avoiding storms altogether, it's about facing them with confidence and emerging stronger. By applying these principles, individuals, businesses, and governments can create systems that not only withstand shocks but thrive in the face of challenges. These strategies ensure that money and banking remain tools for growth, stability, and opportunity, even in the most turbulent times.

Conclusion: Key Takeaways and Insights

Weathering economic storms is no easy task, but the principles of financial resilience provide a powerful framework for navigating uncertainty and emerging stronger.

The strategies discussed, building an emergency fund, embracing diversification, managing risks, and fostering adaptability, are not just theoretical ideas; they are proven, practical tools that have repeatedly helped individuals, businesses, and governments overcome challenges.

When these principles are applied thoughtfully, they serve as a shield against the unpredictable nature of economic cycles, enabling financial systems to endure shocks and recover with greater strength.

For individuals, resilience starts with preparation.

An emergency fund may seem like a simple concept, but its impact during a crisis cannot be overstated. It provides not only a financial buffer but also peace of mind, allowing people to face uncertainties without the added burden of financial stress. Diversification further amplifies this security, reducing vulnerability by spreading risk across multiple income streams or investments. These habits of saving and planning connect back to earlier themes explored in this book, underscoring how the choices we make today lay the foundation for long-term stability.

Businesses, too, demonstrate the power of resilience when they adopt strategies like diversifying operations, managing cash flow effectively, and leveraging innovative solutions. Companies that plan for uncertainty, rather than reacting to it, are often better positioned to adapt when disruptions arise. The importance of these practices was evident during the COVID-19 pandemic, where businesses that embraced digital transformation or adjusted their supply chains were more likely to survive and even thrive. These stories highlight how businesses, like individuals, must prioritize adaptability as a cornerstone of resilience.

Governments play an even broader role in fostering resilience on a systemic level.

Policies such as unemployment benefits, stimulus packages, and infrastructure investments not only stabilize economies during downturns but also build trust in public institutions. Without trust, even the most well-designed interventions can fall flat, as citizens and businesses hesitate to engage with financial systems. The importance of trust has been a recurring theme throughout this book, and nowhere is it more critical than in the relationship between governments and their citizens during times of crisis.

The need for systemic resilience is further magnified by the interconnectedness of today's global economy. Systemic risks, such as banking collapses, cyberattacks, or widespread supply chain disruptions, require collaboration among governments, businesses, and individuals to address effectively.

Interconnectedness means that resilience in one part of the system often supports stability in others.

For example, innovations in financial technology, such as blockchain or predictive analytics, are playing a transformative role in creating more robust and adaptive systems capable of withstanding shocks on a global scale.

Blockchain, with its decentralized and transparent nature, enhances security and efficiency in transactions, while predictive analytics allows institutions to anticipate risks and respond proactively. These advancements not only reduce vulnerabilities by improving the resilience of financial systems but also open up new opportunities for growth and inclusion, particularly by expanding access to banking services in underserved regions and enabling more efficient global trade.

Adaptability remains a central theme in financial resilience.

In a world of rapid technological advances, geopolitical changes, and global challenges like climate change, those who can pivot quickly are more likely to succeed. Individuals must continuously develop new skills, businesses need to remain agile in their operations, and governments must anticipate future risks and opportunities. Adaptability is not just about survival, it is about fostering innovation and transformation in the face of uncertainty.

Sustainability is another pillar of resilience, offering a pathway to long-term stability by addressing environmental and social challenges.

Economies built on sustainable practices are less vulnerable to resource shortages or market volatility. Green initiatives, such as renewable energy projects and sustainable financial products, demonstrate that ethical decisions and practical strategies can align to create a more equitable future. These efforts reflect the interconnected goals of economic resilience, trust, and innovation.

The lessons of financial resilience are critical because they reveal a profound truth about the economics of banking and money: success breeds success.

When individuals, businesses, and governments demonstrate resilience, they build momentum. This momentum strengthens trust in financial systems, inspiring further innovation and progress. A bank that supports a struggling community during tough times creates lasting loyalty and confidence. A government that implements effective policies during a crisis reinforces the public's belief in its ability to lead. Success has a compounding effect, creating a virtuous cycle where trust and stability reinforce one another.

As we turn to the next chapter, we'll explore real-world success stories that illustrate the transformative power of resilience and innovation. These stories will show how small victories can lead to significant progress, demonstrating why success is not just about surviving challenges but thriving in their aftermath. Success is critical because it fosters the trust and momentum needed to build stronger, more inclusive financial systems.

By examining these examples, we gain a deeper appreciation for the role that success plays in shaping the future of money and banking.

CHAPTER 12: Success Stories

Amid the many challenges that economies and financial systems face, there are always shining examples of success, stories that remind us of the resilience, innovation, and adaptability that define the best of human ingenuity. These stories illustrate how effective financial strategies, diversification, and well-executed plans can turn potential crises into opportunities for growth and stability. They are a testament to the power of planning and the importance of adapting to change, themes that have resonated throughout this book.

Consider how some economies have navigated through turbulent times with innovative policies.

Iceland

During the global financial crisis of 2008, as economies around the world spiraled into recession and banking systems faced collapse, a few nations emerged as case studies in resilience, each adopting unique approaches to navigating the crisis. Among these, Iceland stands out as a striking example of bold and unconventional decision-making. While many countries chose to prop up failing financial institutions through massive bailouts, Iceland took a different, controversial path: it allowed its three largest banks, Glitnir, Landsbanki, and Kaupthing, to fail. This radical decision, though painful in the short term, set the stage for a remarkable recovery and serves as a powerful lesson in the importance of decisive action during times of economic turmoil.

The crisis hit Iceland particularly hard. Its banking sector, which had grown exponentially in the years leading up to 2008, was disproportionately large compared to the size of its economy. When the global financial system began to falter, Iceland's banks found themselves over-leveraged and unable to meet their obligations. The government, faced with the enormous costs of bailing out these institutions, chose instead to let them collapse. This decision was not without consequence. The immediate aftermath saw significant economic contraction, a sharp rise in unemployment, and a steep decline in the value of Iceland's currency, the krona.

However, Iceland's bold choice also brought unexpected benefits. By refusing to assume the massive debts of its banks, the government avoided the long-term fiscal burdens that many other countries faced as a result of their bailout strategies.

Instead of transferring private-sector losses to taxpayers, Iceland protected its public finances, allowing the nation to focus on rebuilding its economy from the ground up. The government also implemented capital controls to stabilize the krona and introduced measures to restructure household debt, providing relief to its citizens and restoring a sense of fairness and trust in the system. This approach required significant sacrifices.

The immediate economic pain was severe, and Iceland faced international criticism for its decisions.

However, by prioritizing long-term recovery over short-term fixes, the nation set itself on a path to stability and growth. Within a few years, Iceland's economy began to recover, buoyed by a combination of tourism, exports, and strong public policy. Its ability to rebuild trust, both among its citizens and in the eyes of the international community, proved critical to its resurgence.

Iceland's story underscores the importance of bold, decisive action in the face of financial crises. It also highlights the role of trust as a cornerstone of economic recovery. By addressing systemic weaknesses directly and prioritizing fairness, Iceland demonstrated that even the most devastating crises can become opportunities for reinvention. This case serves as a reminder that resilience often requires difficult decisions and a willingness to challenge conventional wisdom. Iceland's recovery offers valuable lessons for nations, businesses, and individuals about the power of determination and the importance of trust in rebuilding from the ground up.

The United Arab Emirates

Diversification has long been recognized as a cornerstone of financial resilience, not only for individuals and businesses but also for entire economies. The ability to spread risks across multiple sectors and sources of revenue can mean the difference between vulnerability to external shocks and long-term stability.

One of the most striking examples of this principle in action is the transformation of the United Arab Emirates (UAE). Once heavily dependent on oil exports for its economic prosperity, the UAE has undertaken a remarkable journey toward diversification, reshaping its economic landscape and setting an example for other resource-rich nations.

In the mid-20th century, oil exports were the lifeblood of the UAE's economy, fueling rapid development and unprecedented wealth. However, as the global oil market became increasingly volatile and concerns about the long-term sustainability of fossil fuels grew, the UAE recognized the risks of relying too heavily on a single industry. Fluctuations in oil prices, geopolitical instability, and the eventual transition to renewable energy posed significant challenges to economies overly dependent on oil revenues. These concerns prompted the UAE to chart a bold new course, investing heavily in diversifying its economy to reduce its vulnerability to oil market shocks.

Over the past few decades, the UAE has made significant strides in developing alternative sectors, transforming itself into a global hub for tourism, technology, finance, and trade.

Cities like Dubai and Abu Dhabi have become synonymous with luxury tourism, offering world-class attractions, iconic landmarks, and an unparalleled blend of culture and modernity. At the same time, the UAE has established itself as a leader in technology and innovation, fostering start-ups, embracing artificial intelligence, and investing in smart city infrastructure to future-proof its economy. The finance sector has also flourished, with the UAE emerging as a key player in global banking and investment, further solidifying its position as a diversified economic powerhouse.

These efforts have not only provided new streams of revenue but have also created a more stable and sustainable economic environment.

By diversifying its economic base, the UAE has reduced its exposure to the inherent risks of oil dependency and created opportunities for long-term growth. This shift has allowed the nation to weather periods of low oil prices with greater resilience and has positioned it to remain competitive in a world increasingly focused on sustainability and innovation.

The UAE's success story underscores the importance of diversification as a universal principle of resilience. It highlights how strategic investments in multiple sectors can protect against the volatility of any single market, ensuring a more balanced and adaptable economy. This lesson applies equally to nations, businesses, and individuals. Whether it's an economy building multiple pillars of growth, a business expanding its product lines, or an individual diversifying investments, the fundamental goal remains the same: to minimize risks and maximize opportunities.

Ultimately, the UAE's transformation offers a blueprint for how economies can prepare for the uncertainties of the future. By reducing reliance on a single industry and embracing innovation, nations can create more robust and sustainable systems capable of thriving even in the face of global challenges. Diversification is more than just a financial strategy, it is a pathway to resilience, adaptability, and long-term success.

Mobile Banking In Africa

Innovation in banking has been a driving force behind some of the most remarkable success stories in modern finance, particularly in fostering financial inclusion across underserved regions. In parts of the world where traditional banking systems have historically been out of reach for large segments of the population, innovative technologies have stepped in to bridge the gap. One of the most striking examples of this is M-Pesa, a mobile banking platform launched in Kenya in 2007. What started as a simple solution for transferring money has grown into a transformative tool that has reshaped the financial landscape for millions of people across Africa.

M-Pesa operates through mobile phones, allowing users to save, borrow, transfer, and manage money without needing access to a bank account. For many in Kenya, where banking infrastructure was limited and inaccessible to rural or low-income populations,

M-Pesa provided a lifeline. By eliminating the need for brick-and-mortar branches or complex account requirements, it democratized financial services, giving people an opportunity to participate in the economy in ways that were previously unimaginable.

The impact of M-Pesa has been profound.

For individuals, it has provided a secure and convenient way to save money, manage expenses, and even access credit. This has been particularly transformative for rural communities and small business owners, who previously relied on informal and often unreliable methods of managing their finances. With M-Pesa, entrepreneurs can now access microloans to start or expand businesses, enabling local economies to grow and thrive. For women, who are often disproportionately excluded from financial systems, M-Pesa has been a powerful tool for economic empowerment, giving them control over their finances and the means to support their families.

Beyond individual users, M-Pesa has had a ripple effect on the broader economy. By streamlining transactions and reducing the costs associated with traditional banking, it has made commerce more efficient and accessible. Small businesses, the backbone of many developing economies, have benefited immensely from the ability to conduct transactions quickly and securely. This has not only boosted local trade but also created new opportunities for economic growth and job creation.

M-Pesa's success has inspired similar initiatives across the globe, particularly in other African nations, where mobile banking platforms have become a key driver of financial inclusion. Countries like Tanzania, Ghana, and Uganda have adopted similar models, expanding access to financial services for millions more people. This wave of innovation has also sparked interest from larger financial institutions and technology companies, which see the potential of mobile banking to reach untapped markets and drive global financial inclusion.

The story of M-Pesa and other mobile banking initiatives highlights how technology can break down barriers and create more equitable financial systems. It underscores the transformative power of innovation in addressing systemic challenges and empowering those who have been left out of traditional economic frameworks. By leveraging technology to bridge gaps, these platforms have not only improved individual livelihoods but have also contributed to more inclusive and resilient economies.

This is a testament to the importance of integrating technology into financial systems, a theme explored in earlier chapters on financial technology.

As we move further into the digital age, the lessons from M-Pesa remind us that innovation is not just about creating new tools; it's about designing solutions that make financial systems more accessible, equitable, and effective for everyone. In doing so, technology has the potential to drive not just financial growth but also societal progress, creating a brighter future for communities around the world.

Post Covid-19 Policies

Government policies play a critical role in building economic resilience and facilitating recovery, especially during times of crisis. The COVID-19 pandemic was a stark reminder of how deeply interconnected public health, economic stability, and social well-being are. In the face of one of the most significant global disruptions in modern history, governments around the world were forced to act swiftly to mitigate the economic fallout.

Countries like New Zealand and Germany stood out for their proactive and targeted measures, which helped protect jobs, support businesses, and stabilize their economies.

Their successes provide valuable lessons on the importance of well-designed policies and the trust citizens place in public institutions during times of uncertainty.

New Zealand, under the leadership of Prime Minister Jacinda Ardern, adopted a decisive and compassionate approach to managing the pandemic. By implementing a comprehensive lockdown early in the outbreak, New Zealand was able to contain the virus effectively, which laid the foundation for a quicker economic recovery. Alongside strict public health measures, the government introduced substantial financial support packages to protect jobs and livelihoods. Wage subsidies were provided to employers to help them retain staff, ensuring that the workforce remained intact even as businesses faced reduced revenue. These measures not only mitigated the immediate impact of the pandemic but also preserved the capacity for a swift rebound as restrictions eased. The government's clear and empathetic communication throughout the crisis fostered public trust, ensuring widespread compliance with health measures and support for economic policies.

Germany, another standout example, leveraged its strong fiscal position and robust social safety nets to cushion the blow of the pandemic. The government implemented a series of targeted stimulus measures, including grants for small businesses, expanded unemployment benefits, and tax relief for struggling sectors. One of Germany's most notable strategies was the Kurzarbeit program, which subsidized wages for workers whose hours were reduced due to the pandemic. This policy prevented mass layoffs, maintaining income stability for millions of households and preserving jobs that would have been difficult to recreate in the recovery phase. Germany's strong healthcare infrastructure and efficient vaccine rollout further accelerated its path to economic stabilization.

Both New Zealand and Germany benefited from a combination of factors that bolstered their resilience: pre-existing robust public institutions, the ability to mobilize resources effectively, and a high level of trust between governments and their citizens. Their examples highlight the importance of well-designed, timely, and transparent policies in addressing crises. When citizens trust their governments to act in their best interests, they are more likely to comply with public health measures and support economic recovery initiatives, creating a virtuous cycle of cooperation and resilience.

These case studies also underscore the interconnected role of governments and central banks in stabilizing economies during crises, a theme explored in earlier chapters.

While fiscal policies provided immediate relief to households and businesses, central banks supported recovery by maintaining low interest rates, injecting liquidity into financial systems, and ensuring the continued flow of credit. Together, these coordinated efforts demonstrate the importance of a holistic approach to crisis management, where monetary and fiscal policies work in tandem to address both short-term needs and long-term recovery.

The successes of New Zealand and Germany also serve as a reminder that resilience is not built overnight. The ability to respond effectively to crises often depends on the groundwork laid during more stable times. Strong healthcare systems, fiscal reserves, and trust in public institutions are all investments that pay dividends during periods of uncertainty. Their experiences offer valuable lessons for other nations on how to prepare for and navigate future challenges.

In times of crisis, the role of governments extends beyond implementing policies, it is about inspiring confidence, fostering solidarity, and demonstrating that collective action can overcome even the most daunting challenges. By combining targeted economic interventions with clear communication and strong public health measures, governments can not only guide their economies toward recovery but also reinforce the trust and cooperation needed to build a more resilient future.

Cooperative Banking

Community-driven financial initiatives have emerged as some of the most compelling success stories in fostering economic resilience, demonstrating the power of collective action and local engagement in building stable financial systems.

Cooperative banking models and credit unions, in particular, stand out as prime examples of how communities can come together to create financial institutions that prioritise the needs of their members over the demands of external shareholders. These community-focused organisations have shown time and again that they are uniquely equipped to weather economic downturns and support local economies through periods of uncertainty.

The success of cooperative banking models lies in their structure and purpose.

Unlike traditional banks, which aim to maximise profits for shareholders, cooperative banks and credit unions are owned and governed by their members, who are also their customers. This member-focused approach creates a fundamentally different set of priorities, with decisions driven by the collective interests of the community rather than the pursuit of short-term financial gains. This model fosters trust and loyalty among members, who know that their financial institution is working for their benefit rather than for external investors.

During economic downturns, this focus on community needs provides cooperative banks and credit unions with a resilience that often outpaces traditional banks. Because these institutions are less focused on high-risk, high-reward investments, they tend to operate with more conservative lending practices and stronger ties to their local economies. This prudent approach helps insulate them from the kind of speculative risks that have led to the collapse of larger financial institutions during crises, such as the 2008 global financial crisis. Moreover, their emphasis on long-term sustainability rather than short-term profits allows them to continue serving their communities even in challenging times.

One of the most significant strengths of cooperative banks and credit unions is their ability to provide tailored support to individuals and businesses during periods of economic uncertainty.

For small businesses, which often struggle to access credit from traditional banks during recessions, these community-driven institutions serve as vital lifelines. They offer loans, financial advice, and other resources designed to help local businesses survive and thrive. For individuals, credit unions often provide more favourable loan terms, lower fees, and higher savings rates than traditional banks, easing the financial burdens that many face during economic downturns.

The local focus of cooperative banks and credit unions also contributes to their resilience and impact. By serving the specific needs of their communities, they create a sense of shared purpose and mutual support that strengthens social bonds and fosters economic stability. For example, during the COVID-19 pandemic, many credit unions around the world stepped up to provide emergency loans, defer payments, and offer financial counselling to their members, helping to mitigate the immediate effects of the crisis. Their ability to adapt quickly and respond to the unique challenges faced by their communities made a significant difference in supporting recovery efforts.

Another advantage of these community-driven initiatives is the trust they inspire among their members.

In times of economic uncertainty, trust is a critical factor in maintaining financial stability, as it influences individuals' willingness to save, borrow, and invest. Cooperative banks and credit unions build this trust by maintaining transparent governance structures, involving members in decision-making processes, and reinvesting profits back into the community. This trust, in turn, strengthens their resilience, as members are more likely to remain loyal and committed to the institution even during difficult times.

The success of cooperative banking models and credit unions underscores the broader importance of inclusivity and collaboration in financial systems. By prioritising the needs of local communities, these institutions not only provide essential services but also empower individuals and businesses to take an active role in shaping their economic futures. Their ability to foster trust, stability, and resilience offers valuable lessons for the financial sector as a whole, particularly as the world faces ongoing challenges such as economic inequality, climate change, and digital transformation.

In an increasingly interconnected world, the principles underlying cooperative banks and credit unions, mutual support, shared responsibility, and a focus on long-term well-being, are more relevant than ever.

These community-driven financial initiatives remind us that resilience is not just about surviving crises; it is about building systems that support collective prosperity and empower individuals to thrive. By embracing these principles, we can create more equitable and sustainable financial systems that truly serve the needs of all.

Green Initiatives

Sustainability is rapidly emerging as a cornerstone of success in the financial world, reshaping the priorities and strategies of banks, investors, and institutions worldwide.

As the global economy faces mounting challenges from climate change, resource depletion, and shifting consumer expectations, the financial sector is increasingly recognizing that aligning with sustainable practices is not only a moral imperative but also a smart business strategy. Investing in green initiatives and renewable energy projects has become a powerful way for financial institutions to contribute to environmental preservation while fostering economic growth and long-term resilience.

One of the most transformative tools in this movement has been the rise of green bonds.

These financial instruments are designed specifically to fund environmentally sustainable projects, such as solar and wind farms, clean transportation systems, and energy-efficient infrastructure. By channeling capital into these initiatives, green bonds have become a critical driver of the transition to a low-carbon economy. Governments, corporations, and financial institutions alike have embraced green bonds as a means to finance projects that address environmental challenges while also generating economic opportunities.

The impact of green bonds is far-reaching. For example, solar farms funded through green bonds have not only helped reduce greenhouse gas emissions but have also created jobs and supported local economies. Clean transportation systems, such as electric buses and high-speed rail networks, have improved urban mobility while reducing air pollution and dependence on fossil fuels. By focusing on projects that deliver both environmental and economic benefits, green bonds are helping to build a more sustainable and equitable future.

Financial institutions are also expanding their involvement in sustainable finance beyond green bonds.

Many banks are now incorporating environmental, social, and governance (ESG) criteria into their investment and lending decisions. By prioritizing companies and projects that meet high sustainability standards, these institutions are driving positive change across industries. This shift has also been fueled by growing demand from investors, who increasingly view ESG-compliant investments as not only ethical choices but also as lower-risk, higher-reward opportunities in the long term.

The emphasis on sustainability has extended to renewable energy projects, which have become a focal point for both public and private investment. From wind farms in Europe to solar power installations in Africa and Asia, renewable energy projects are providing clean, reliable power to millions of people while reducing reliance on fossil fuels. Financial institutions have played a key role in financing these projects, often working in partnership with governments and development organizations to ensure their viability and scalability.

The growing commitment to sustainability in the financial sector reflects a broader understanding of the interconnectedness of economic, environmental, and social systems.

By investing in green initiatives, financial institutions are helping to address some of the most pressing challenges of our time, from climate change to inequality. These efforts also align with the long-term goals of creating a financial system that is not only resilient but also forward-looking, adaptable, and inclusive.

Sustainability is not just a trend; it is becoming a defining feature of the financial world. Institutions that fail to adapt risk being left behind as the global economy continues to shift toward more sustainable practices. On the other hand, those that embrace sustainability are positioning themselves as leaders in a rapidly changing landscape, capable of driving innovation, fostering trust, and delivering value to stakeholders.

Ultimately, the integration of sustainability into the financial system represents a profound shift in how we think about the role of finance in society. It moves us beyond the traditional focus on short-term profits to consider the broader impact of financial decisions on the planet and future generations. By investing in green initiatives and renewable energy, financial institutions are not only contributing to a more sustainable world but are also laying the foundation for long-term economic stability and prosperity. This alignment of economic and environmental goals is a powerful testament to the potential of finance to drive meaningful change, proving that a resilient financial system can also be a sustainable one.

Conclusion: Key Takeaways and Insights

These success stories remind us that while challenges are inevitable, they are far from insurmountable. History shows us that resilience, diversification, innovation, and trust are not merely theoretical concepts, they are powerful, actionable strategies that have consistently turned adversity into opportunity. Whether it's a country rebuilding its financial systems after a crisis, a business adapting to a changing market, or a community uniting to create local solutions, success creates momentum.

Momentum, once achieved, has a way of compounding itself, inspiring further progress and building trust along the way.

Trust is the backbone of every financial system, and success has an undeniable way of reinforcing it. When a bank performs well, whether by supporting businesses with loans, managing risks effectively, or investing in local economies, the ripple effects are felt far and wide. Individuals gain confidence in their financial institutions, businesses feel secure enough to grow and hire, and governments can rely on stable systems to fund public services. In this way, the success of banks becomes a shared success, lifting entire communities and economies.

Momentum builds as trust strengthens, creating a virtuous cycle. A bank that funds a small business today may see that business thrive and expand, generating profits, creating jobs, and ultimately reinvesting in the local economy. That growth feeds back into the banking system, creating new opportunities for lending and investment. Similarly, an innovative government policy or financial product that succeeds in solving a localized problem can inspire adoption on a broader scale, turning small victories into global best practices. These examples demonstrate how success can spark further success, creating an environment where prosperity becomes more accessible and sustainable for all.

But this momentum relies on the willingness of institutions and individuals to embrace adaptability and forward-thinking strategies. It's not enough to achieve success; it must be nurtured and leveraged to navigate the inevitable challenges that lie ahead. Financial systems, like the people and businesses they serve, must constantly evolve to stay resilient. Whether that means adopting new technologies, expanding access to underserved populations, or preparing for the next global disruption, the ability to anticipate and adapt is essential to maintaining the trust and stability that success requires.

Success stories also teach us that resilience and innovation are not one-time achievements but ongoing commitments. The economic systems that thrive are those built on a foundation of trust and guided by principles that prioritize long-term sustainability over short-term gains. This idea of shared success is why strong, well-functioning banks are so crucial, not just for the financial sector, but for society as a whole. When banks do well, we all do well. They are the engines of growth, fueling everything from individual dreams to national economies, and their ability to maintain trust and stability benefits everyone.

As we reflect on the lessons explored so far, it becomes evident that success in money and banking extends beyond solving today's challenges, it demands foresight, adaptability, and the courage to innovate. The financial systems we build must not only withstand the pressures of the present but also anticipate and address the complexities of the future.

Resilience, innovation, and trust remain the cornerstones of sustainable economic progress, driving societies toward greater stability, inclusivity, and prosperity.

In this next chapter, we introduce you to the intriguing and often misunderstood world of shadow banking. Unlike traditional banking, shadow banking operates in the financial system's periphery, offering services and solutions that banks either cannot or will not provide.

From hedge funds to money market funds, from asset-backed securities to repurchase agreements, shadow banking has evolved into a crucial yet opaque part of the global financial ecosystem.

CHAPTER 13: Shadow Banking

Shadow banking sounds mysterious, almost ominous, doesn't it? The term might conjure images of secret transactions happening in dimly lit rooms, but the reality is both less dramatic and far more impactful.

Credit, Liquidity, and Funding

Shadow banking refers to financial activities and entities that operate outside the traditional banking system and its regulations. Hedge funds, money market funds, and structured investment vehicles are just a few examples. While these entities don't accept deposits like traditional banks, they play a crucial role in providing credit, liquidity, and funding to the global economy. This world of shadow banking operates in parallel with the traditional banking system but with its own set of rules, or often, the lack of them.

Early on, I want to say this: shadow banking is a vast and complex topic, deserving its own detailed exploration. In fact, one of my future books will delve deeply into its intricacies, risks, and opportunities. That said, it's impossible to fully understand the dynamics of money and banking without touching on the role of shadow banking.

It's a different world but one that's intrinsically linked to the financial systems we've discussed throughout this book. So, consider this chapter a primer, a glimpse into the hidden engine that keeps many aspects of the financial system humming.

One reason it's called "shadow banking" is its lack of regulation compared to traditional banks.

These entities and activities exist in the gray spaces of financial oversight. While this allows for innovation and flexibility, it also introduces risks. The 2008 financial crisis, for instance, shone a spotlight on shadow banking. Complex financial instruments, such as collateralized debt obligations (CDOs), were central to the crisis, and many were facilitated outside the purview of traditional banking. This lack of transparency created vulnerabilities that rippled through the global economy when things unraveled.

Higher Risk Loans and Niche Markets

Despite its challenges, shadow banking is vital to the financial world. It provides credit and liquidity in areas where traditional banks might hesitate, such as high-risk loans or niche markets. Think about it:

when traditional banks tighten their lending practices during an economic downturn, shadow banking often steps in to fill the gap. This flexibility can stabilize markets and keep the wheels of commerce turning, especially in sectors where access to capital is critical.

Market Makers

Market makers, particularly dealers, are integral to the functioning of shadow banking. Dealers help create liquidity by buying and selling financial instruments, often in markets that are too complex or volatile for traditional players. For example, in the realm of derivatives, contracts whose value depends on the performance of underlying assets, dealers play a crucial role in ensuring these instruments can be traded efficiently. This ability to provide liquidity helps reduce market volatility and supports broader economic activity, even if most people aren't directly aware of it.

Risk and Reward

What makes shadow banking so intriguing is how it straddles the line between risk and reward. On one hand, its innovations often lead to efficiencies and opportunities that traditional banking simply cannot provide. On the other hand, the opacity of shadow banking can amplify systemic risks, particularly when markets experience stress. For instance, during the COVID-19 pandemic, some shadow banking entities faced liquidity crises that threatened broader financial stability. These moments underscore the need for a balance between innovation and oversight, a recurring theme throughout this book.

Fairness and Access

Shadow banking also raises questions about fairness and accessibility. While it has driven significant financial innovation, much of its activity is concentrated in advanced economies and among large institutional players. This raises the question: how can the benefits of shadow banking be made more inclusive, extending its impact to smaller businesses and developing economies? Answering that question might involve rethinking regulatory frameworks, but as with traditional banking, trust and transparency are key.

Looking to the future, shadow banking is poised to evolve alongside advancements in financial technology.

Blockchain and decentralized finance (DeFi), for instance, could reshape shadow banking by making it more transparent and accessible, or, conversely, by introducing new complexities and risks. How these technologies are adopted and regulated will play a major role in determining the future of shadow banking's role in the global economy.

Conclusion: Key Takeaways and Insights

It's clear that shadow banking is not just a peripheral player in the world of money and banking, it is a critical, albeit often misunderstood, pillar of the financial system. Operating outside the spotlight, it drives innovation, expands access to credit, and provides the elasticity needed to respond to the demands of a dynamic global economy.

Shadow banking's ability to adapt and innovate makes it a powerful force.

This enables the creation of credit and liquidity where traditional banks may hesitate. This flexibility has allowed markets to evolve rapidly, fostering economic growth and enabling opportunities in ways that regulated banking systems alone could not achieve.

However, the very characteristics that make shadow banking so impactful also introduce significant risks.

Operating outside the oversight of traditional banking regulation, shadow banking can become a source of instability, especially during times of financial stress. The elasticity of credit that shadow banking provides is a double-edged sword. While it enables rapid expansion of the money supply to meet growing economic demands, it also creates vulnerabilities when confidence erodes. A sudden contraction in shadow banking credit can have cascading effects, leading to liquidity crises and amplifying economic downturns. Striking the right balance between flexibility and regulation will be essential as we navigate the complexities of shadow banking in the future.

Understanding shadow banking also means recognizing its profound impact on the elasticity of money.

Unlike traditional banks, which are limited by reserve requirements and regulatory constraints, shadow banking expands the effective money supply through securitization, repo markets, and other mechanisms. This elasticity allows economies to grow by providing much-needed credit in times of high demand. However, this same mechanism also underscores the importance of trust and transparency. Without them, the very system that supports economic growth can become a source of instability, as witnessed during the 2008 financial crisis.

As we reflect on shadow banking's role, it becomes clear that its success, like that of traditional banking, rests on three foundational principles: trust, innovation, and adaptability. Trust ensures that markets function smoothly and that participants have confidence in the system. Innovation drives progress, creating new opportunities for economic growth and inclusion. Adaptability allows the system to respond to changing conditions, ensuring resilience in the face of uncertainty. These principles are not only central to shadow banking but are also themes that have resonated throughout this book.

While this chapter provides a glimpse into the fascinating and complex world of shadow banking, the topic demands a deeper exploration.

That's why I plan to dedicate another book entirely to shadow banking. In it, we will explore how shadow banking has evolved, the mechanisms that make it work, and the risks and rewards it presents to the global economy. We'll examine its critical role in market making, its impact on credit creation, and its relationship with traditional banking. Shadow banking is a world unto itself, and understanding its intricacies is vital for anyone seeking a comprehensive view of modern financial systems.

As we approach the final chapter of this book, it's important to reflect on how shadow banking connects to the broader themes we've discussed. From the evolution of money to the role of banks, the interconnectedness of financial systems has been a recurring theme. Shadow banking exemplifies this interconnectedness, operating alongside traditional banks and influencing credit, liquidity, and the flow of money in profound ways.

It's a reminder that no part of the financial system exists in isolation, and every element, from regulated banks to the shadowy corners of finance, plays a role in shaping economic stability and growth.

In the last chapter, we'll tie all these themes together in a robust reflection on the evolution of money and banking. We'll consider what the future of money might look like in 10, 20, or even 50 years, exploring the possibilities that lie ahead in a world shaped by trust, innovation, and adaptability.

Most importantly, we'll discuss the role you, the reader, can play in shaping that future.

The choices we make today, whether as individuals, businesses, or policymakers, will determine the trajectory of our financial systems. Together, we'll consider how we can create a world where money and banking continue to serve as tools for growth, stability, and opportunity for generations to come.

CHAPTER 14: Conclusion and Reflection

Pause and Reflect

As we reach the final chapter of this journey, it's time to pause and reflect on the incredible landscapes we've explored together. From the ancient barter systems to the digital currencies of today, money has proven to be a mirror of human innovation and trust.

Summary of Chapters

In Chapter One, we saw how the earliest forms of trade laid the foundation for economic systems.

The leap from trading goods directly to creating universally accepted forms of money was more than just a practical solution, it was a testament to our ability to build systems that require collective belief.

Banks, as we discussed in Chapter Two, are much more than vaults safeguarding our wealth.

They serve as the lifeblood of economies, channeling resources from savers to borrowers and creating credit that drives progress. But with that power comes responsibility. We explored how fractional reserve banking amplifies the impact of deposits, while also posing risks that require careful regulation.

It's fascinating to think about how something as mundane as a bank account can underpin entire economies.

Money flows through our lives like a river, as we examined in Chapter Three.

Supply and demand determine its course, while individual decisions ripple outward to influence larger markets. Spending and saving are personal acts, yet they collectively shape inflation, deflation, and overall economic activity. This interplay reminds us that economics is not just about numbers, it's about choices, behaviour, and balance.

Central banks, which we unravelled in Chapter Four, wield immense influence as the invisible hands of the economy.

By adjusting interest rates and controlling the money supply, they steer nations toward stability. Whether it's the Federal Reserve or the European Central Bank, these institutions operate behind the scenes to ensure growth, even if their actions sometimes spark controversy. Their role underscores the importance of trust in maintaining economic harmony.

Chapter Five delved into the booms, busts, and crises that have defined financial history.

Of course, history has shown us that economic harmony is fragile. From the 2008 financial meltdown to earlier banking collapses, we saw how cycles of greed, risk, and mismanagement can lead to disaster. Yet, there's hope in the recovery strategies that emerge, proof that resilience is as much a part of our economic story as crisis.

On a global scale, money transcends borders, shaping trade and power dynamics, as explored in Chapter Six.

Foreign exchange markets, trade imbalances, and currency valuations are not just technical terms, they're the mechanisms that connect nations. The movement of money globally is a reminder that we are all part of a larger economic web, with opportunities and challenges shared across continents.

Technology, the star of Chapter Seven, is rewriting the rules of money and banking.

Blockchain, cryptocurrencies, and digital banking are more than buzzwords, they're the building blocks of a new financial world. The potential of these innovations is boundless, but they also challenge us to rethink trust, regulation, and accessibility. The future isn't just arriving, it's being invented in real-time.

Speaking of the future, Chapter Eight offered a glimpse into what lies ahead.

From sustainable banking practices to financial technologies that enhance transparency, the path forward is filled with promise. But as always, trust remains the cornerstone. Innovation is only as impactful as the systems of belief that support it.

On a more personal note, Chapter Nine examined the psychology of money.

Why do we spend, save, or invest the way we do? Behavioural economics reveals how our decisions are shaped by emotion and cognitive biases. Understanding these influences allows us to navigate financial decisions more wisely, turning what might feel irrational into opportunities for growth. Not all stories of money and banking are positive.

Chapter Ten took us into the shadows, exposing scandals, corruption, and crime.

These darker chapters of history remind us of the importance of regulation and transparency. Trust, once broken, is hard to rebuild, but it's essential to the integrity of financial systems.

Resilience, as highlighted in Chapter Eleven, is the key to weathering economic storms.

Whether it's individuals building emergency funds or governments managing recessions, the ability to adapt and recover defines success. Practical examples of diversification and risk management showed us how to prepare for uncertainties while maintaining hope for the future.

The uplifting stories of financial resilience in Chapter Twelve provided a balance to the challenges discussed earlier.

Success stories from individuals, businesses, and economies proved that overcoming adversity is possible. These examples inspire us to believe in the power of perseverance and smart decision-making.

Finally, Chapter Thirteen introduced the concept of shadow banking.

Though complex and often misunderstood, this parallel financial system plays a crucial role in modern economies. By teasing the topic, we hinted at the broader worlds waiting to be explored, a reminder that the journey of learning never truly ends.

Your Journey Continues

The journey doesn't end here. The concepts explored in this book, particularly in the final chapters on shadow banking and emerging future trends, are just the beginning of a much larger conversation. Shadow banking, for instance, unveils an entire parallel realm of financial mechanisms that operate outside traditional banking systems. From hedge funds to securitized lending markets, this shadow world is not only fascinating but also crucial to understanding the complexities of modern finance. While these topics have been touched on here, they serve as an invitation for deeper investigation, offering countless opportunities to explore how these systems function and how they impact global financial stability.

As you close this book, I encourage you to see it not just as an endpoint but as a springboard for further discovery.

Reflect on the insights gained about the evolution of money and banking, the intricacies of economic systems, and the innovative forces shaping the financial landscape. These pages have covered a wide array of topics, from the historical foundations of banking to the transformative power of financial technology, the importance of resilience, and the promise of sustainability. Yet, the financial world is ever-evolving, and new challenges and opportunities continue to emerge. Let this book serve as both a reflection on where we've been and a guide for where we are headed.

My hope is that these chapters have sparked your curiosity, inspired thoughtful questions, and provided a foundation of knowledge that will enrich your understanding of the financial world. Whether you are a student, a professional, or simply someone with an interest in the dynamics of money and banking, I hope this book has equipped you with the tools to navigate the complexities of economics with greater confidence and insight.

The financial world is vast and interconnected, with each concept a thread in a much larger tapestry. The lessons we've explored here, about trust, resilience, innovation, and sustainability, are not confined to banking and economics; they extend to all aspects of life, from personal decision-making to global collaboration. As you continue your journey, I encourage you to seek out the stories, systems, and ideas that lie beyond these pages. Dive deeper into shadow banking, explore the implications of financial technology, and consider the profound role of sustainability in shaping the future of economies.

Thank you for taking this journey with me. Writing this book has been an opportunity to share not only knowledge but also my passion for understanding the forces that shape our financial world. My hope is that you will carry this passion forward, applying what you've learned to your own pursuits and contributing to a more informed and empowered society.

May your ongoing exploration of economics, money, and banking be one of discovery, growth, and success.

Whether you delve into advanced studies, share these insights with others, or use them to inform your own financial decisions, know that you are part of a larger conversation about how we can build systems that are resilient, equitable, and sustainable. The path ahead is full of opportunities, and I wish you the very best as you continue to learn, grow, and succeed.

Let this be the start of a lifelong journey of curiosity and exploration, one that leads to greater understanding and meaningful contributions to the world around us.

Updated List of Books to Date

Willem Tait is the author of several impactful real estate books that examine the dynamic and ever-changing nature of the real estate market. Each book provides valuable strategies, practical insights, and a comprehensive understanding of the key factors influencing the industry. Below is the full list of his published works to date:

Real Estate Law Essentials: Navigate Cross-Sections, Avoid Pitfalls, and Seize Opportunities. A comprehensive guide to understanding the legal frameworks surrounding real estate, offering practical advice for navigating transactions and mitigating risks.

Proven Principles of Residential Real Estate Investment: Strategies and Tasks for Building Generational Wealth. A detailed exploration of residential real estate investment strategies, designed to help readers achieve long-term financial security and success.

Practical Principles of Commercial Real Estate Investment: Tasks and Strategies for Real Estate Success. Focused on commercial real estate, this book provides actionable principles and strategies for navigating the complexities of the market and achieving professional growth.

Real Estate Economics: Property Market Principles and Practices. This book offers an informative, in-depth analysis of real estate markets, their practices and their underlying principles, and the economic forces driving them.

Raising Money for Real Estate Investment: Close Deals, Raise Money, Build Wealth. A practical guide to securing funding for real estate projects, this book emphasizes effective deal-making and wealth-building strategies.

Capital Markets and Real Estate: Bridging Markets for a Global Future. This work explores the intersection of real estate and capital markets, highlighting their convergence and the opportunities that globalization presents for industry professionals.

Real Estate Development and Deal Making: The Essential Guide for Property Developers, Entrepreneurs, and Dealmakers. This comprehensive guide ties together the foundational principles of property development with innovative strategies for deal-making and entrepreneurship, providing actionable insights for success in the industry.

Psychology of Residential and Commercial Real Estate: Master the Psychology Behind Real Estate Success. A practical guide into real estate decision making. By uncovering the emotions, motivations, and cognitive biases behind property decisions, this book provides actionable strategies for property success.

Philosophy of Residential and Commercial Real Estate: Exploring the Intersection of Philosophy, People, Property, Purpose and Spaces. A thoughtful exploration of the deeper meaning behind property and spaces. By examining the beliefs, values, and purposes that shape real estate, this book provides insightful principles for aligning property decisions with vision and intent.

Economics of Banking and Money: Explores how money and banking shape modern economies. From currency's origins to digital finance, it demystifies complex topics and connects them to daily life. An essential guide for students and curious readers, it shows how trust and innovation drive finance.

Real Estate Mastery Books Series

These books are part of the Real Estate Mastery Books, a series designed to equip readers with the tools and knowledge necessary to excel in the fields of real estate and capital markets. This ever-expanding series reflects Willem Tait's commitment to providing actionable insights and strategies. Keep an eye out for upcoming titles in this growing collection, as there are always more exciting additions to come.

Acknowledgement

I am deeply humbled and grateful for the incredible support and encouragement I received throughout the creation of this book. To my teachers and professors, thank you for imparting your knowledge and challenging me to think critically. Your lessons have left an indelible mark on my journey.

To my peers and business partners, your collaboration and insights have been invaluable. Your willingness to share your perspectives enriched this work in ways I could not have achieved alone. I am especially grateful to those who made themselves available for interviews, your openness and generosity with your time and expertise added depth and authenticity to these pages.

This book is a reflection of collective effort, and I am honored to have had the guidance and support of so many along the way. To everyone who contributed in any way, big or small, thank you from the bottom of my heart.

Social Profiles

Willem Tait is committed to staying connected and engaging with his readers. He is active on LinkedIn and X (formerly Twitter), where he shares updates on his latest projects, insights, and resources. Willem is also available for face-to-face consultations, public speaking, and group training sessions through platforms like WhatsApp, Zoom, Google Meet, and Microsoft Teams.

Feel free to reach out on any of these platforms to connect, share ideas, or discuss opportunities for learning and growth. Let's keep building together!

LinkedIn: https://www.linkedin.com/in/willemtait/
X (previously Twitter): https://x.com/willemtait
Calendly: https://calendly.com/willemtait
Email: willemtait@outlook.com

Mentorship, Coaching, Consulting and Public Speaking

As a dedicated professional with a passion for real estate, business, law, and economics, I thrive on sharing actionable insights and practical strategies that empower individuals and teams to achieve their goals. My expertise spans real estate investment, business consulting, personal growth, and the intricate connections between legal and economic frameworks, allowing me to offer a well-rounded perspective tailored to diverse challenges and ambitions.

Through public speaking engagements, customised mentorship programs, and dynamic one-on-one or group coaching sessions, I aim to inspire, educate, and guide. Whether addressing an audience of hundreds or working closely with a small team, my mission is to deliver value-driven insights that leave a lasting impact.

If you're seeking a keynote speaker to energise and inform your event, a consultant to elevate your business strategies, or a mentor to foster personal and professional growth, I'm here to collaborate. My approach integrates years of hands-on experience with a solid foundation in real estate, law and economics, ensuring the strategies I share are both practical and informed by robust principles.

Let's connect to explore how I can help you or your organisation unlock new opportunities and achieve meaningful success. Together, we can create strategies that inspire growth, drive innovation, and deliver measurable results.

LinkedIn: https://www.linkedin.com/in/willemtait/

Mail: willemtait@outlook.com

About the Author

Willem Tait is an accomplished author, real estate expert, and industry mentor whose journey through the worlds of property investment, real estate development, capital markets, and human understanding has inspired professionals across the globe. With decades of experience, Willem has become a trusted voice in real estate strategy, capital markets integration, and the transformative power of mentorship, all underpinned by a deep interest in psychology, philosophy, and the profound connections between people and spaces.

Willem's passion for education, critical thinking, and professional growth is reflected in the nine insightful books authored to date. Each work delves into the intricate dynamics of real estate while exploring the psychological and philosophical forces that shape decision-making and human interaction. Offering practical strategies, actionable insights, and thought-provoking perspectives, Willem's writings span topics from sustainability and innovation to navigating complex financial landscapes. This prolific body of work solidifies his position as an authority in the field, bridging the gap between theory, practice, and the human experience with clarity and expertise.

Beyond writing, Willem Tait holds a strong academic foundation, having pursued advanced studies that inform a nuanced understanding of real estate, economics, psychology, and philosophy. This dedication to lifelong learning complements a hands-on approach to mentoring aspiring professionals, helping them achieve their goals in real estate and beyond. Known for his ability to break down complex concepts into accessible knowledge, Willem empowers readers and mentees alike to navigate the evolving challenges of the industry while fostering a deeper understanding of the motivations and principles that drive success.

Whether guiding readers through the intricacies of capital markets, exploring the philosophical meaning of spaces, or inspiring the next generation of leaders, Willem Tait continues to shape the conversation around real estate and its future. This blend of expertise, passion, and a commitment to human connection ensures that Willem remains not just a specialist, but a trailblazer in the ever-changing world of real estate, capital markets, and the broader human narrative.

We Value Your Feedback!

Thank you for taking the time to read this book. Your insights and experiences with this book mean the world to me, and I would love to hear your thoughts.

If you found the strategies and principles in this book helpful, please consider leaving a review on Amazon or your preferred platform. Your feedback not only helps me improve but also helps other readers discover valuable resources for their commercial real estate journey.

Sharing your thoughts can inspire others to take the next step in their investment journey. Whether it's a quick rating or a detailed review, your voice makes a difference!

Thank you again for your time and trust in this book. Wishing you success in all your real estate ventures!

Portfolio of Books by Willem Tait

For more, kindly see www.amazon.com/author/willemtait

BUSINESS BOOKS

1. **Real Estate Law Essentials:** Navigate Cross-Sections, Avoid Pitfalls, and Seize Opportunities.
2. **Proven Principles of Residential Real Estate Investment:** Strategies and Tasks for Building Generational Wealth.
3. **Practical Principles of Commercial Real Estate Investment:** Tasks and Strategies for Real Estate Success.
4. **Real Estate Economics:** Property Market Principles and Practices.
5. **Raising Money for Real Estate Investment:** Close Deals, Raise Money, Build Wealth.
6. **Capital Markets and Real Estate:** How Money and Capital Shapes the Property Market.
7. **Real Estate Development and Deal Making:** The Essential Guide for Property Developers, Entrepreneurs, and Dealmakers.
8. **Psychology of Residential and Commercial Real Estate:** Master the Psychology Behind Real Estate Success.
9. **Philosophy of Residential and Commercial Real Estate:** Exploring the Intersection of Philosophy, People, Property, Purpose and Spaces.
10. **Economics of Banking and Money:** Insight into Power, Trust, and Change.
11. **The Future of Real Estate:** PropTech, Sustainability and Design

SELF-HELP AND MOTIVATIONAL BOOKS

1. **Sort Your Crap Out:** Own Your Choices, Silence Your Critic. Get Stuff Done
2. **Dammit, Get It Together:** Stop Making Excuses and Start Living the Life You Deserve
3. **Stop Giving a Damn and Start Living:** Cut the Crap. Focus on What Matters. Live Fully
4. **Dammit, It's Your Life:** Own Your Mind, Time, and Choices
5. **Dammit, Stop Being Overwhelmed and Overworked:** Reclaim Your Time, Energy, and Sanity

ANNOTATED AND COMMENTARY

1. **The Way to Wealth** (Annotated): With Motivational Commentary by Willem Tait
2. **The Art Of War:** (Annotated): Proven Modern Strategies for Winning in Business, Leadership, and Life by Willem Tait

Thank you!

In the beginning I said, "This book reveals where money comes from and how to grow it. Join me on a journey of discovery, manipulation, and strategy. You'll thank me later."

I sincerely believe this book has already begun to change your life and will continue to do so. The knowledge shared here is rare. When you truly understand how money is made, where it comes from, and how it is used, you place yourself in a position of power. Very few people ever gain that understanding. Thank you for choosing to be one of them.

Willem Tait

www.ingramcontent.com/pod-product-compliance
Lightning Source LLC
Chambersburg PA
CBHW070954240526
45469CB00016B/869